T0012675

First published in 2024 by Hungry Tomato Ltd.
F15, Old Bakery Studios, Blewetts Wharf,
Malpas Road, Truro, Cornwall, TR1 1QH, UK.

Thanks to our creative team:
Editor: Holly Thornton
Senior Designer: Amy Harvey

Copyright © 2024 Hungry Tomato Ltd

No part of this publication may be reproduced, stored in a retrieval system, or transmitted in any form or by any means, electronic, mechanical, photocopying, recording, or otherwise, without prior written permission of the copyright owner.

A CIP catalog record for this book is available from the British Library.

ISBN: 9781914087684
Printed and bound in China

Discover more at
www.hungrytomato.com
www.mybeetlebooks.com

BUILD IT! MAKE IT!
SPACE

CONTENTS

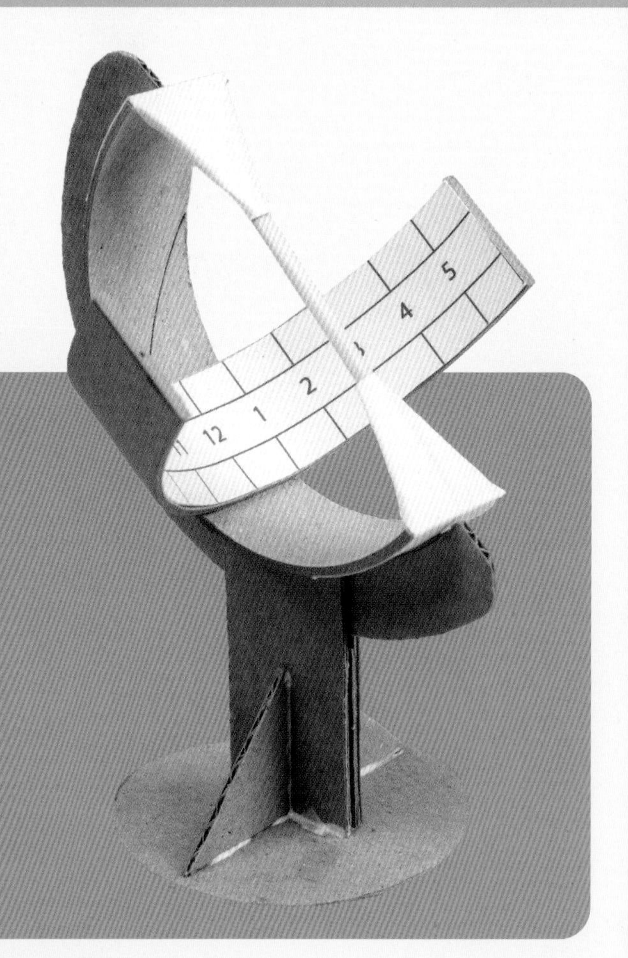

INSTRUMENTS TO STUDY SPACE

AWESOME MODEL SPACECRAFT

WORDS IN **BOLD** CAN BE FOUND IN THE GLOSSARY

CONTENTS

AMAZING SPACE EXPERIMENTS

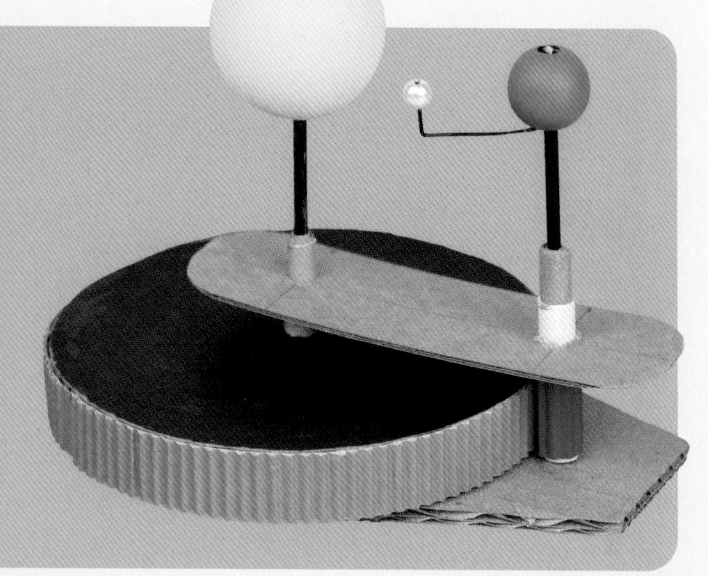

SPECTACULAR SPACE PROJECTS

PREPARE FOR LIFTOFF

Try your hand at building amazing space-themed models! Using smart and simple engineering principles, you can make a whole collection of out-of-this-world crafts that hover, fly, move, and show the wonders of our universe and beyond!

THIS BOOK IS INTERACTIVE!

Some of the projects in this book come with templates to help you cut pieces to the right shape and size. Use a smartphone to scan the QR code at the beginning of the project to access a downloadable template that you can print out.

You will find QR codes at the end of some projects, too. These will direct you to videos of the moving models in action!

You can also find all templates and videos at:
www.mybeetlebooks.com/build-it-make-it-space

PREPARE FOR LIFTOFF

TOP TIPS

- Before you start any project, read the step-by-steps all the way through to get an idea of what you are aiming for. The pictures show what the steps tell you.
- When printing templates, check that your printer is set to "print to scale" or to "full size" to make sure they come out the right size for your other materials!
- Use a cutting mat, or similar surface, for cutting lengths of craft sticks, skewers, and anything else you may need.
- Use the sharp end of a pencil to make small holes in cardboard (see page 11 for method) or ask an adult to help, using either scissors or a craft knife.
- Ask an adult to help straighten out and shape paper clips using a pair of pliers.
- Where strong glue is required, you may want to use a glue gun. Make sure you ask permission, and do not use it without an adult present. Strong liquid glue, such as wood or epoxy glue, will work well, too.

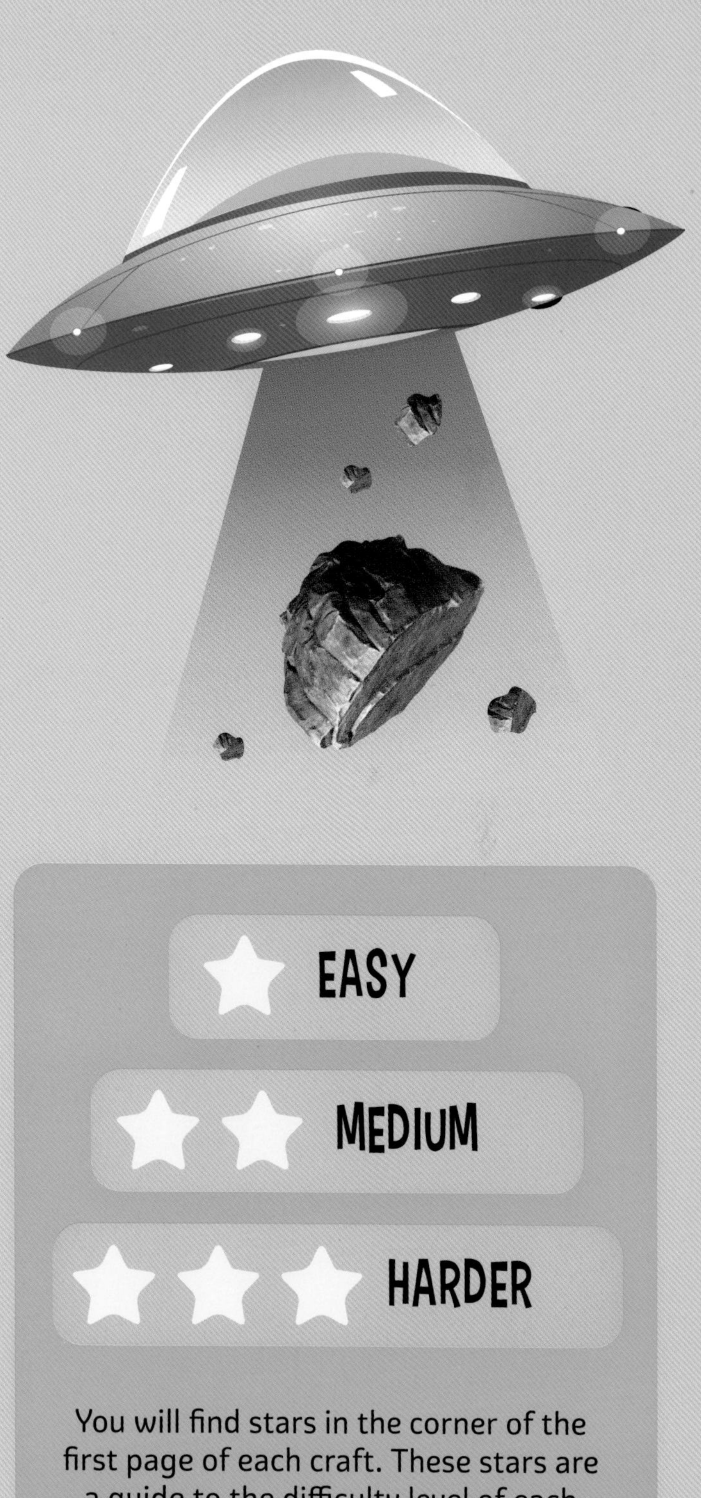

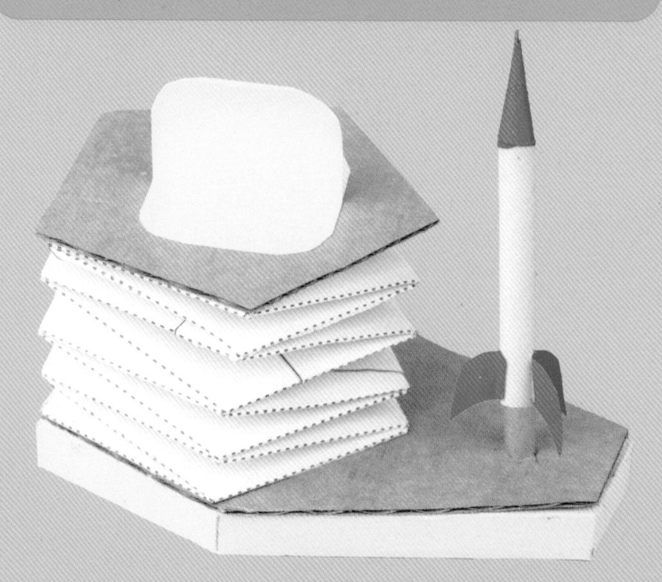

EASY

MEDIUM

HARDER

You will find stars in the corner of the first page of each craft. These stars are a guide to the difficulty level of each project. They show you when you may need another pair of hands!

SAFETY FIRST!

Be careful and use good sense when making these models. They are easy to understand but will require some cutting, gluing, drilling, and other awkward tasks that you may need some help with from an adult.

WHEN TO GET HELP

Watch out for this sign throughout the book. You may need help from an adult when completing these tasks.

DISCLAIMER

The author, publisher, and bookseller cannot take responsibility for your safety. When you make and try out the projects, you do so at your own risk. Look out for the safety warning symbol (shown left) given throughout the book and call on adult assistance when you are cutting materials or using a pair of scissors or pliers, craft drill, or hot glue.

HOW TO CUT A POSTER TUBE SAFELY:

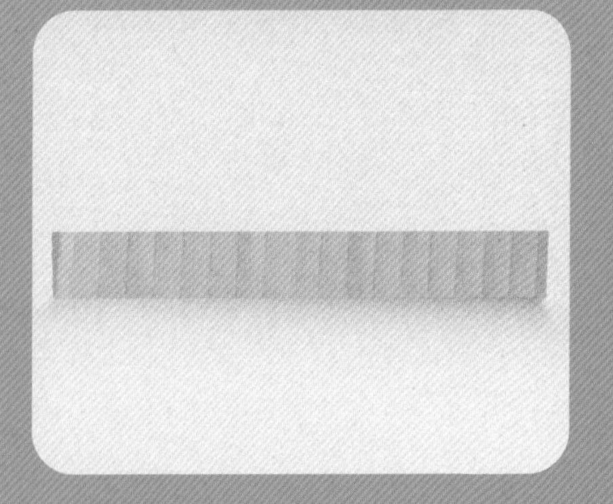

1.
Cut a strip of cardboard and fold a right angle into it. Measure from the crease the width you need the tube to be and make a hole at that point.

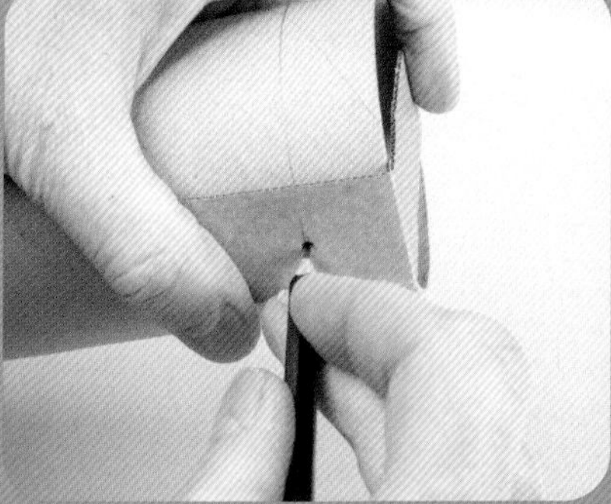

2.
Hold the cardboard over the end of the poster tube. With a pencil in the hole, twist the tube around to draw a line parallel to the edge.

3.
Ask an adult to carefully cut along the line to make a short section of tube. They could use scissors or a craft knife.

SAFETY FIRST!

HOW TO SCORE PAPER OR CARDSTOCK SAFELY:

Using a ruler as a guide, press along the line with a hard plastic item, like the end of a pen lid. Do this on a cutting mat to protect the surface you're working on.

HOW TO MAKE HOLES IN CARDBOARD SAFELY AND EASILY:

INSTRUMENTS TO STUDY SPACE

Humans have studied outer space for centuries. In fact, scientists have found cave drawings of the Sun and stars which date back tens of thousands of years!

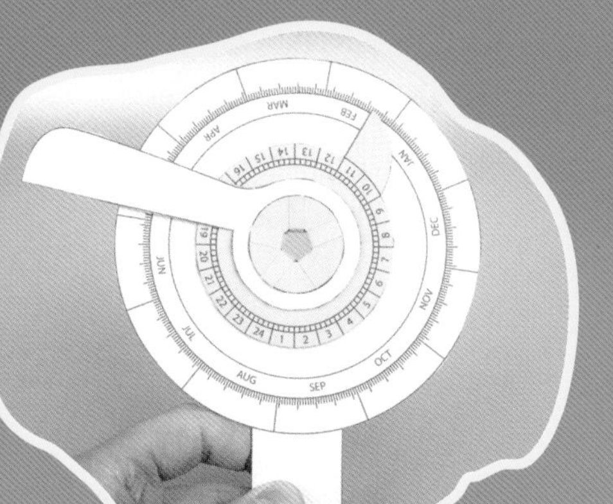

OBSERVING SPACE

The first **astronomers** – people who studied outer space – didn't have the technology we have today. They relied on their eyes to observe the movements of the Sun, Moon, and stars. They noticed patterns in these movements and found clever ways to record them.

TELESCOPE DISCOVERY!

For years, we thought that the Sun **orbited** Earth. It wasn't until the 1600s, when telescopes were used to see faraway planets, like Jupiter, that we discovered all planets in the solar system orbit the Sun. This discovery was a real breakthrough!

WANT TO KNOW MORE?

This chapter is full of fantastic projects which will allow you to conduct your own studies of space. Turn the page to dive in - who knows what you'll discover?

INCLINOMETER

The inclinometer is a scientific instrument used to work out the height of stars in the sky by measuring the angle between the star and the horizon.

WHAT YOU NEED:

- Thread/thin string
- Toothpick
- Thick cardstock/card
- Bulldog clip
- Paper straw ¼ inch (6mm)
- Glass bead ¼ inch (6mm)

TOOLS:

- Pencil
- Semi-circular (180 degree) protractor
- Pair of scissors
- Ruler
- Glue gun (cool melt) or strong craft glue
- Push pin or small craft drill

1 Trace the shape of your protractor onto thick cardstock/card and cut out.

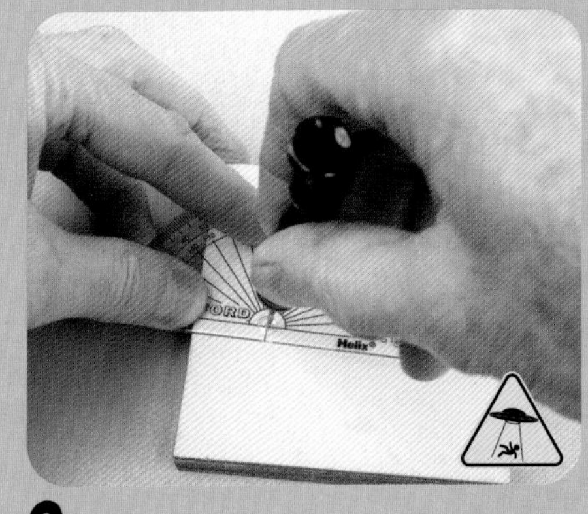

2 Ask an adult to make a fine hole in the protractor at the middle point using a push pin or small craft drill.

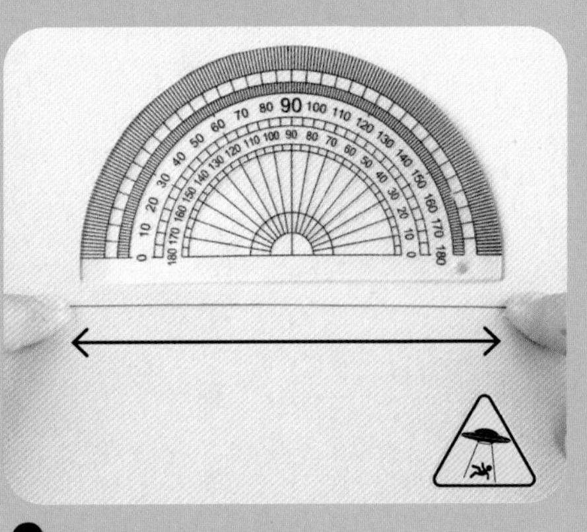

3 Cut a piece of thread/thin string to the length of the base of the protractor.

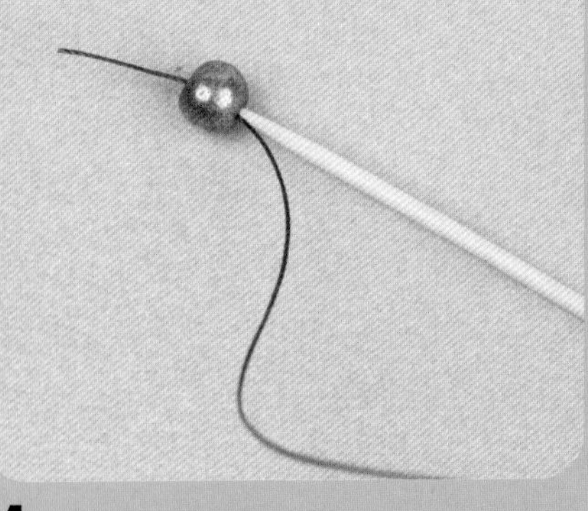

4 Push the thread/thin string through the bead. Secure it in place by pushing a toothpick into the hole.

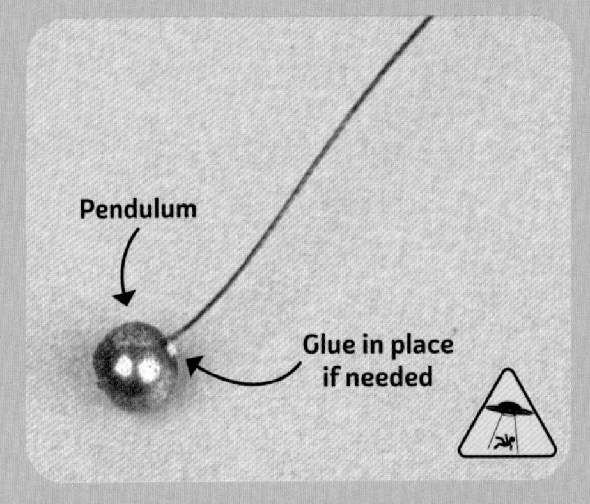

5 Using scissors, carefully cut off the excess toothpick, leaving the tip inside the bead as shown. This bead will be your pendulum.

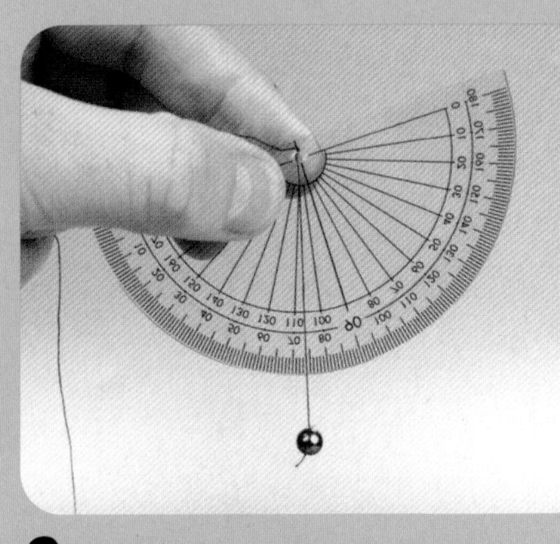

6 With the bead hanging down the back of the protractor, push the thread/thin string through the hole.

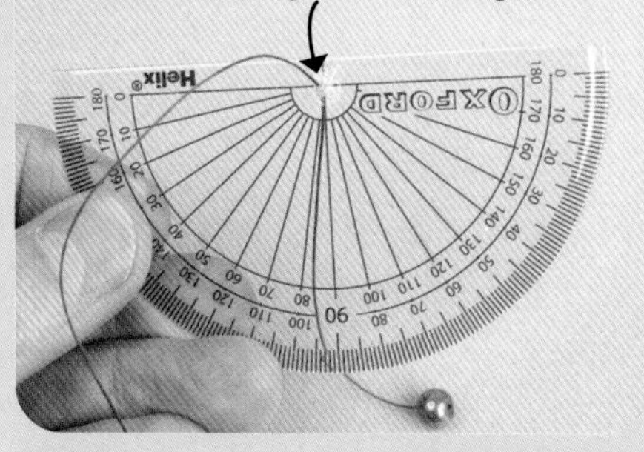

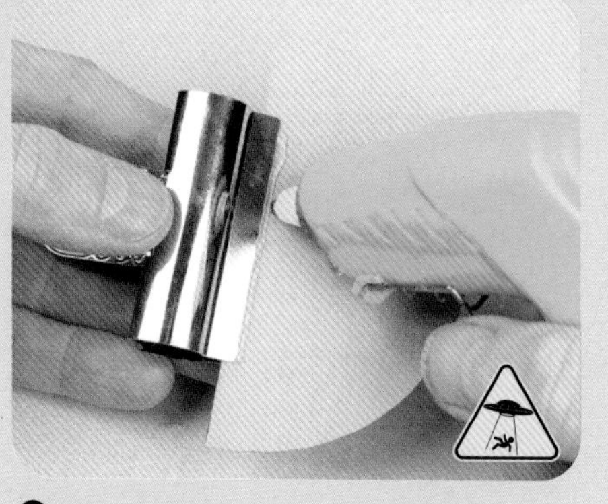

7 Measure the thread so it's 1 inch (25mm) longer than the protractor's radius. Then, glue over the hole to secure.

8 Cut off any excess thread. Then, grip the protractor with the bulldog clip, gluing the front jaw along the length of the protractor.

9 Fit the cardboard semi-circle in place at the back of the protractor. Glue it to the back bulldog jaw to sandwich the pendulum.

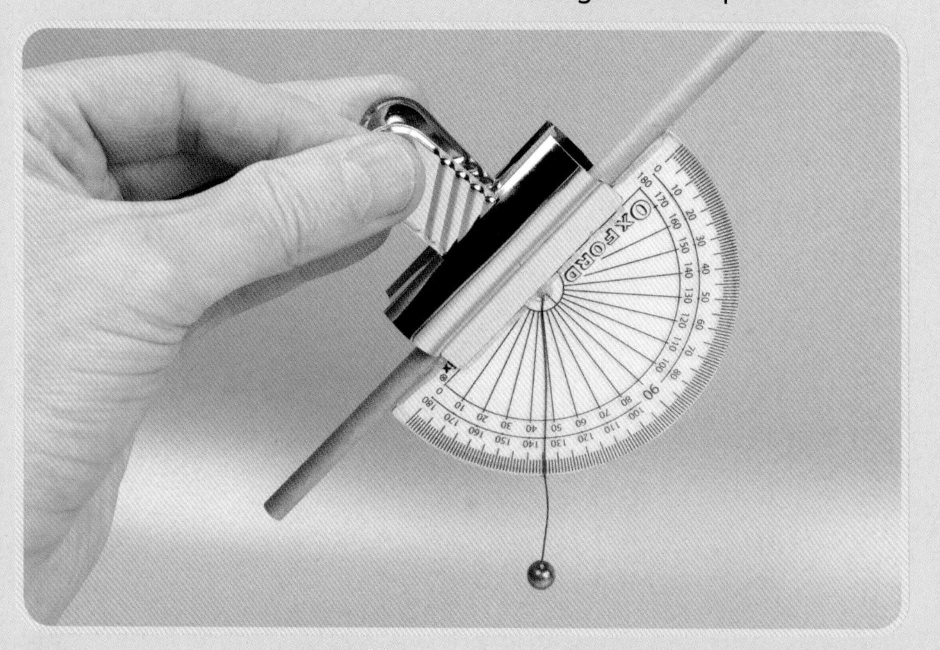

10 Thread the paper straw through the bulldog clip so that its middle roughly lines up with the middle of the protractor.

How to use your inclinometer:

1. Squeeze the bulldog clip so that the pendulum hangs free.

2. Sight the star you're measuring through the straw.

3. Release the bulldog clip to trap the thread.

4. Read the protractor angle that the pendulum is lined up with.

5. Subtract this number from 90 to get the star's inclination.

DID YOU KNOW?

Inclinometers have been used for centuries: they're vital when using the stars to navigate, making maps of the sky, and recording star positions.

MOON PHASES

Watch the progression of the phases of the Moon in super speed with this mini model.

Use the QR code to access the template you need.

WHAT YOU NEED:

- Poster tube 3 inches (80mm) in diameter
- Ping pong/table tennis ball
- Corrugated cardboard
- Assorted cardstock/card
- Bamboo skewer

TOOLS:

- Pencil and eraser
- Black marker pen
- White marker pen
- Ruler
- Pair of scissors
- Strong craft glue
- Craft drill

TOP TIP

If you don't have a poster tube, you could use a wide masking tape roll!

1 Print, copy, or trace the shapes from the template onto the specified materials and cut out.

2 Ask an adult to cut a ring out of a poster tube (see page 10). It needs to be as wide as the ping pong/ table tennis ball.

3 Cut a strip of corrugated cardboard half the width of the tube and long enough to wrap around the interior completely. Glue it to the inside of the tube. It should be level with the top of the tube and reach halfway down.

4 Paint the inside of the tube without the card insert or use a black marker pen as shown.

5 Fit and glue the inner ring into place against the corrugated cardboard lip.

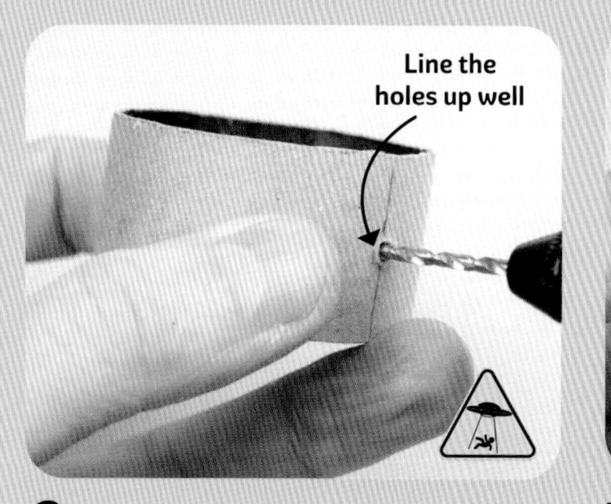

6 Ask an adult to drill a hole halfway down the tube, behind the inner ring. Make another directly opposite.

7 Ask an adult to drill a hole at each end of the ping pong/table tennis ball. They should be on the seam.

8 Cover one half of the ball in black marker pen, using the seam as a guide.

9 Place the ball inside the tube and line up the holes. Then, thread the skewer through the tube and ball. The ball should be free to rotate. Trim the skewer so that ½ inch (13mm) remains at each side.

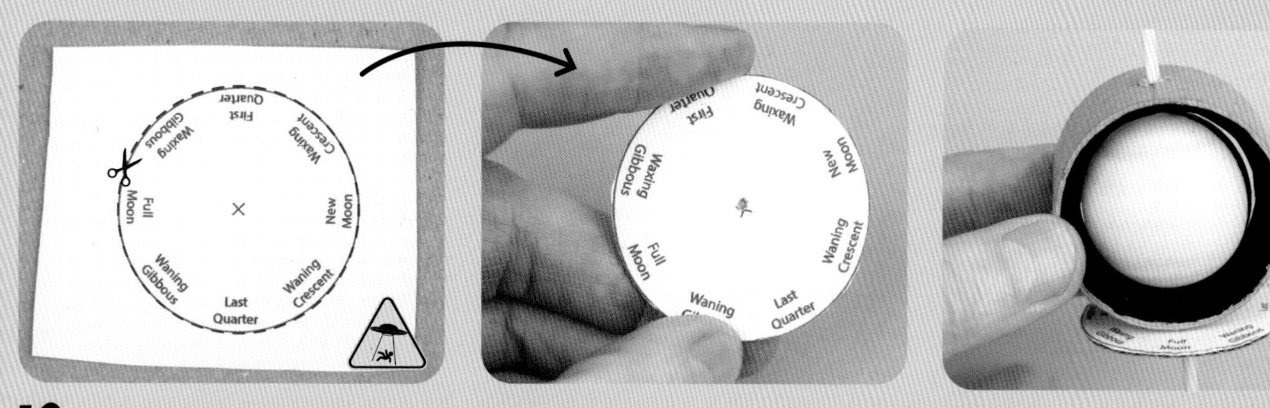

10 Glue the cardstock/card dial from the template to a piece of corrugated cardboard and cut out around the circle. Then, make a hole through the cross in the middle (see page 11).

11 With the text facing up, slide the dial onto the skewer, under the poster tube as shown.

12 Arrange the model so that the black half of the tube, white side of the ball and "full moon" are facing the front.

TOP TIP

The dial and ball should fit perfectly and twist with the skewer. If they don't, you can glue them onto the skewer. Be careful not to glue the poster tube though!

13 Glue the stand legs about halfway up on each side of the poster tube. Make sure that the skewer and dial are off the counter as shown.

Use your own creative space ideas to decorate the outside.

Waxing Gibbous
Last Quarter
Waning Crescent

Regularly check out the phases of the Moon through the months of the year.

ROTATE THE DIAL TO SEE THE DIFFERENT PHASES OF THE MOON!

REFLECTING TELESCOPE

Search for stars, moons, and undiscovered planets with this amazing reflecting telescope. What will you discover?

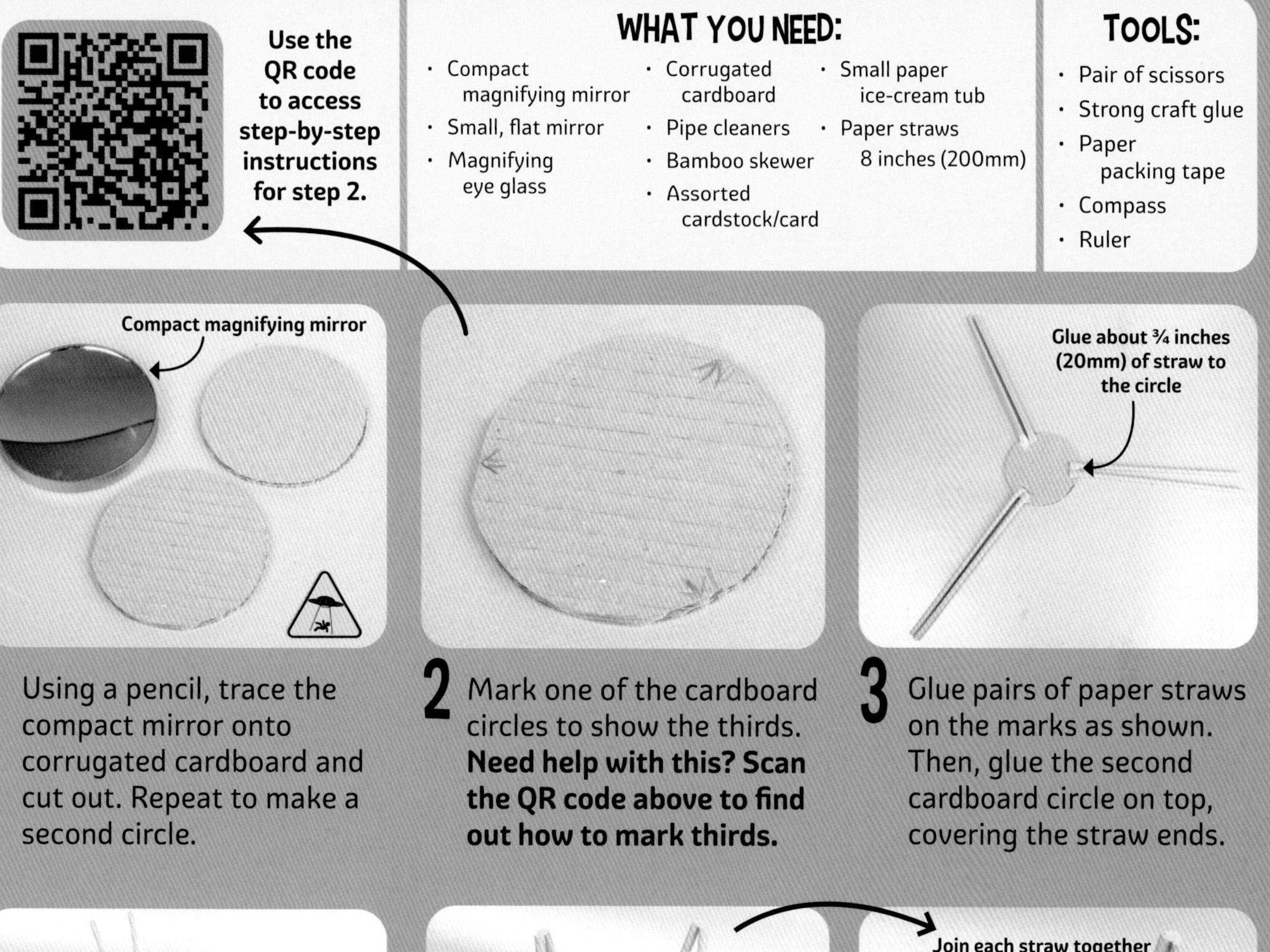

Use the QR code to access step-by-step instructions for step 2.

WHAT YOU NEED:

- Compact magnifying mirror
- Small, flat mirror
- Magnifying eye glass
- Corrugated cardboard
- Pipe cleaners
- Bamboo skewer
- Assorted cardstock/card
- Small paper ice-cream tub
- Paper straws 8 inches (200mm)

TOOLS:

- Pair of scissors
- Strong craft glue
- Paper packing tape
- Compass
- Ruler

1 Using a pencil, trace the compact mirror onto corrugated cardboard and cut out. Repeat to make a second circle.

2 Mark one of the cardboard circles to show the thirds. **Need help with this? Scan the QR code above to find out how to mark thirds.**

3 Glue pairs of paper straws on the marks as shown. Then, glue the second cardboard circle on top, covering the straw ends.

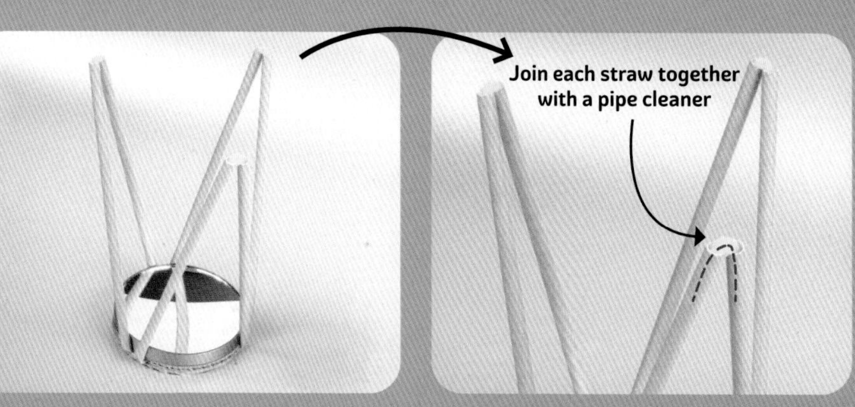

4 With the mirrored side facing up, glue the compact mirror to the top cardboard circle.

5 Connect each straw to the one next to it to create triangle shapes as shown. Insert a pipe cleaner into the straw ends to hold them together.

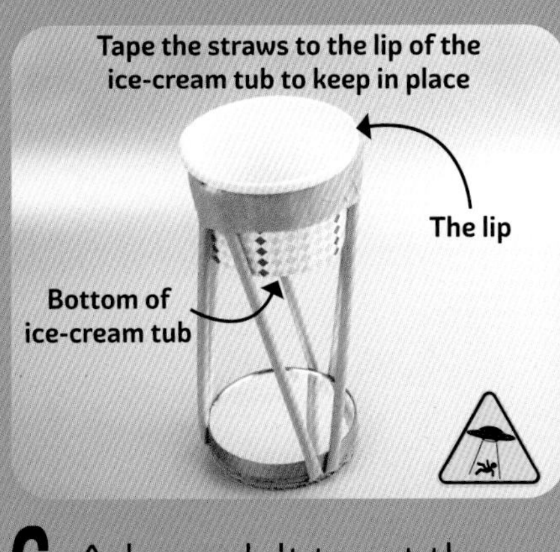

6 Ask an adult to cut the bottom out of the ice-cream tub and place in the middle of the straws and central over the mirror.

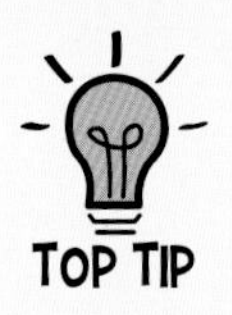

TOP TIP

These craft items are a little bit harder to find. Here's a few ideas of where to look:

- Magnifying compact mirrors can often be found in pharmacies, drugstores, and beauty stores.
- The big magnifying glass lens - used in the Refracting Telescope (page 22) - can often be found online or in thrift stores/charity shops.
- Small magnifying eye glasses can often be found online, or in craft shops and thrift stores/charity shops.

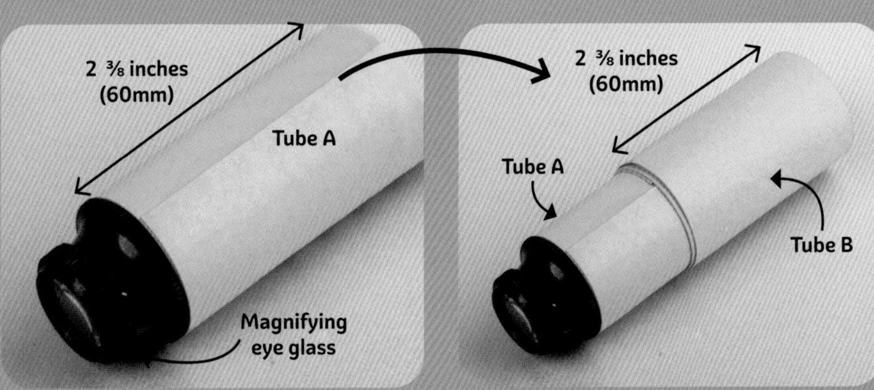

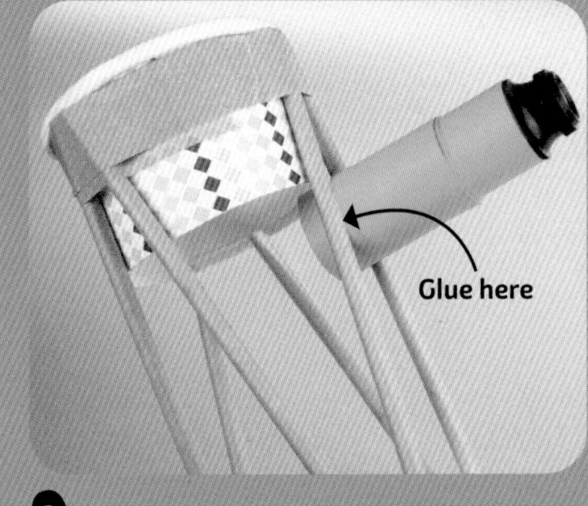

7 Wrap a cardstock/card tube (tube A) tightly around the magnifying eye glass. Glue the loose end down as neatly as possible. Then, make a second tube (tube B) to fit over tube A, as shown, so that they can slide in and out of each other.

8 Glue tube B between two straws, just below the ice-cream tub as shown.

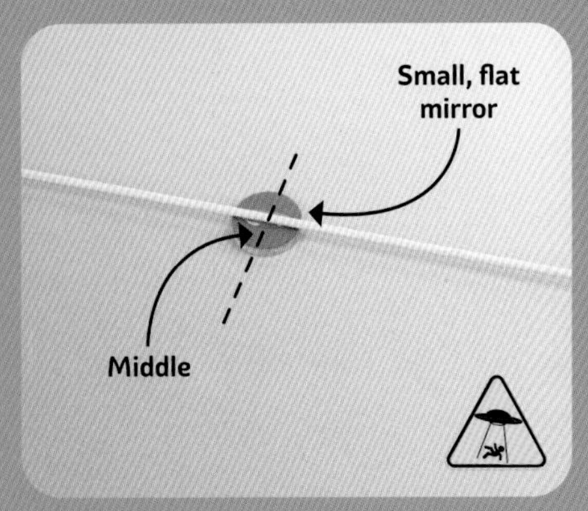

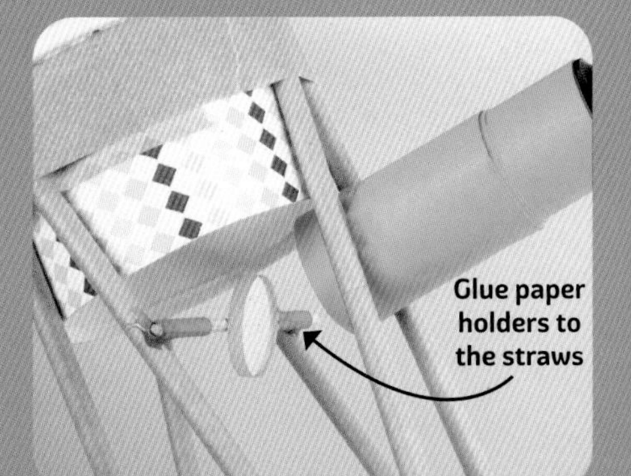

9 Cut a bamboo skewer to 5 ½ inches (140mm) long. Glue the middle of the skewer to the back of the small, flat mirror.

10 Wrap paper tightly around each end of the skewer and glue down the ends. Make sure the skewer can still twist.

11 Position the skewered mirror under the ice-cream tub, facing and in line with the magnifying eye glass, as shown.

How to use your reflecting telescope:

1. Look through the magnifiying eye glass.
2. Adjust the small mirror to the right position so you can see.
3. Pull tube A back and forth to focus the image.

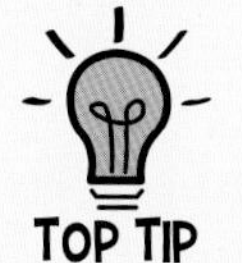

TOP TIP

Remember, it's NEVER safe to look at bright lights or the Sun, so don't point your telescope directly at them.

WHAT CAN YOU SEE?

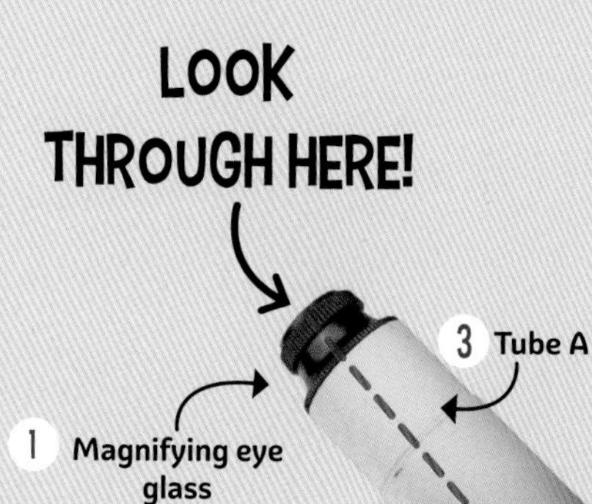

2 Small, flat mirror

DID YOU KNOW?

There are two main types of telescopes: refracting (see page 22) and reflecting, which is best for brighter things like moons and planets.

REFRACTING TELESCOPE

Refracting telescopes are great for seeing things from a long distance. What faraway things can you spot using your amazing refracting telescope?

WHAT YOU NEED:

- Paper cup
- Magnifying glass lens
- Magnifying eye glass
- Poster tube
- Corrugated cardboard
- Assorted cardboard/card

TOOLS:

- Pair of scissors
- Strong craft glue
- Ruler

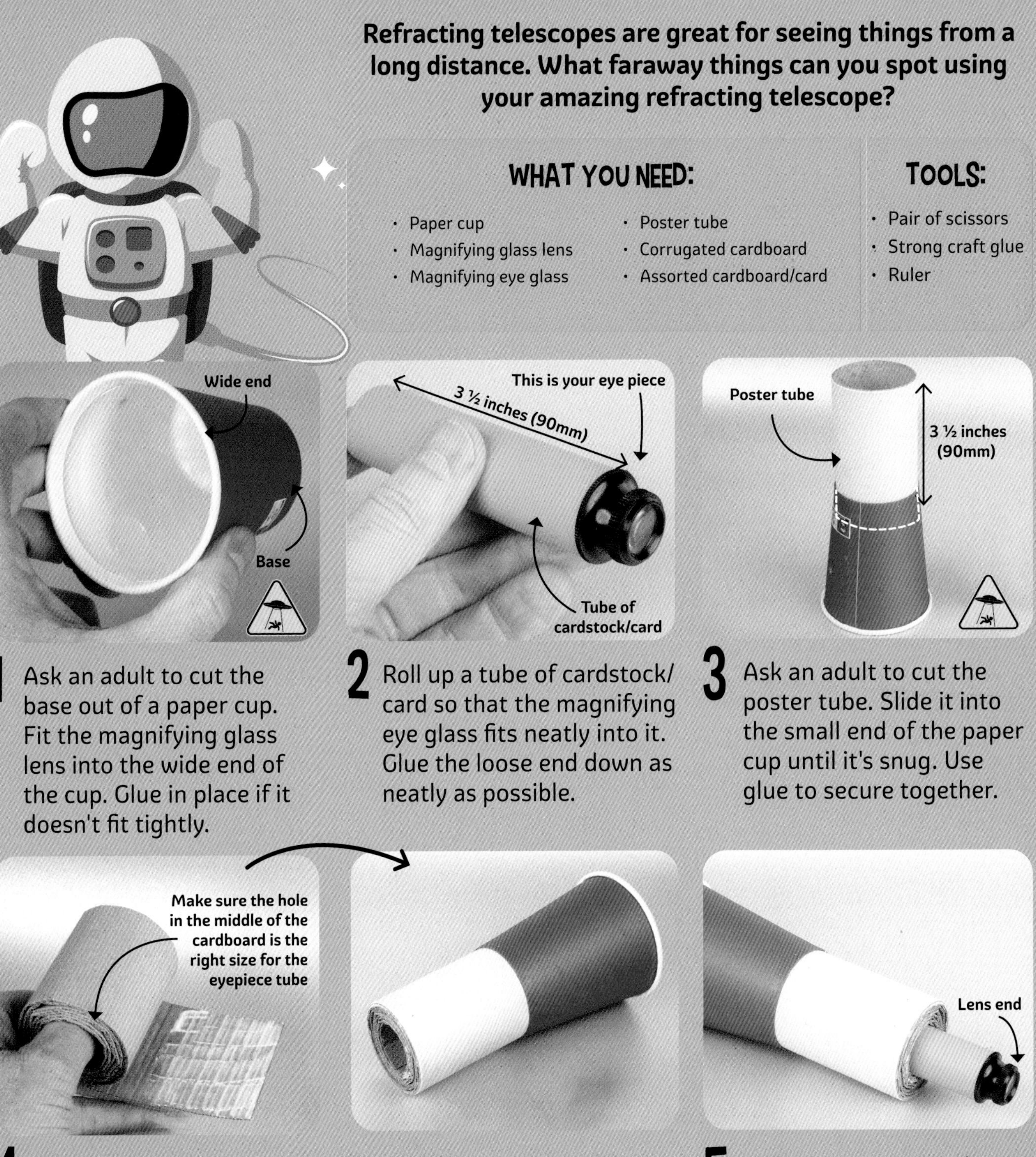

1 Ask an adult to cut the base out of a paper cup. Fit the magnifying glass lens into the wide end of the cup. Glue in place if it doesn't fit tightly.

2 Roll up a tube of cardstock/card so that the magnifying eye glass fits neatly into it. Glue the loose end down as neatly as possible.

3 Ask an adult to cut the poster tube. Slide it into the small end of the paper cup until it's snug. Use glue to secure together.

4 Cut a length of corrugated cardboard that's the same height as the poster tube. Roll up the cardboard, leaving a hole in the middle for the eyepiece, and glue down the end to stop it unravelling. Fit the rolled up cardboard into the poster tube.

5 Slide the eyepiece tube into the hole, with the lens end on the outside. Make sure you can pull the tube in and out to focus.

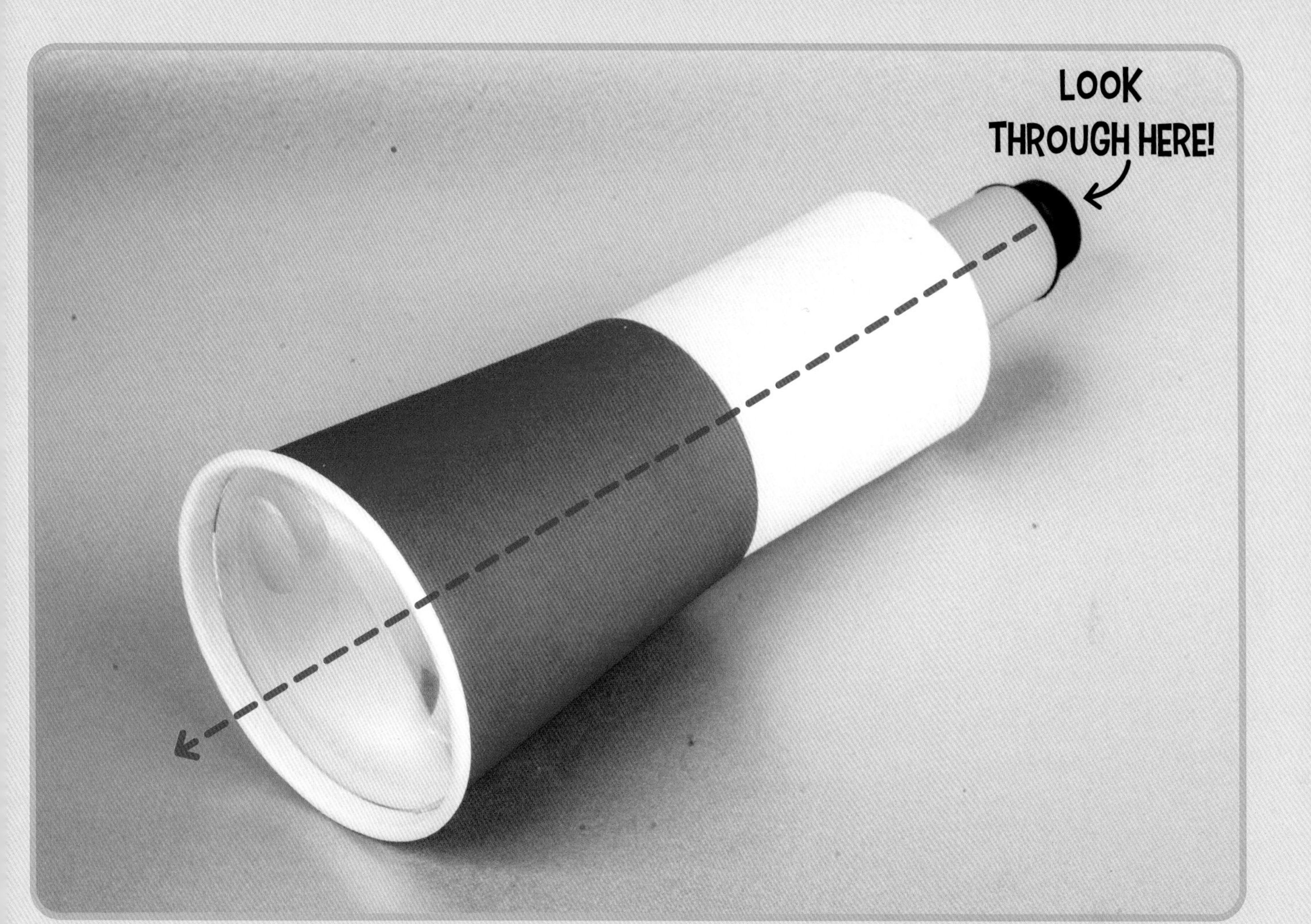

LOOK THROUGH THE EYEPIECE AND PULL THE TUBE IN AND OUT TO FOCUS THE TELESCOPE!

DID YOU KNOW?

Galileo was not the inventor of the telescope, but he was one of the first people to use one to study the sky. He was born in the 1500s and made many discoveries about distant planets, including the rings of Saturn and four of Jupiter's moons! It's thought he used a refracting telescope.

NOCTURNAL TIMEPIECE

This awesome astronomical instrument can be used to tell the time with the stars! Follow the "How to use" guide on the opposite page to do it yourself.

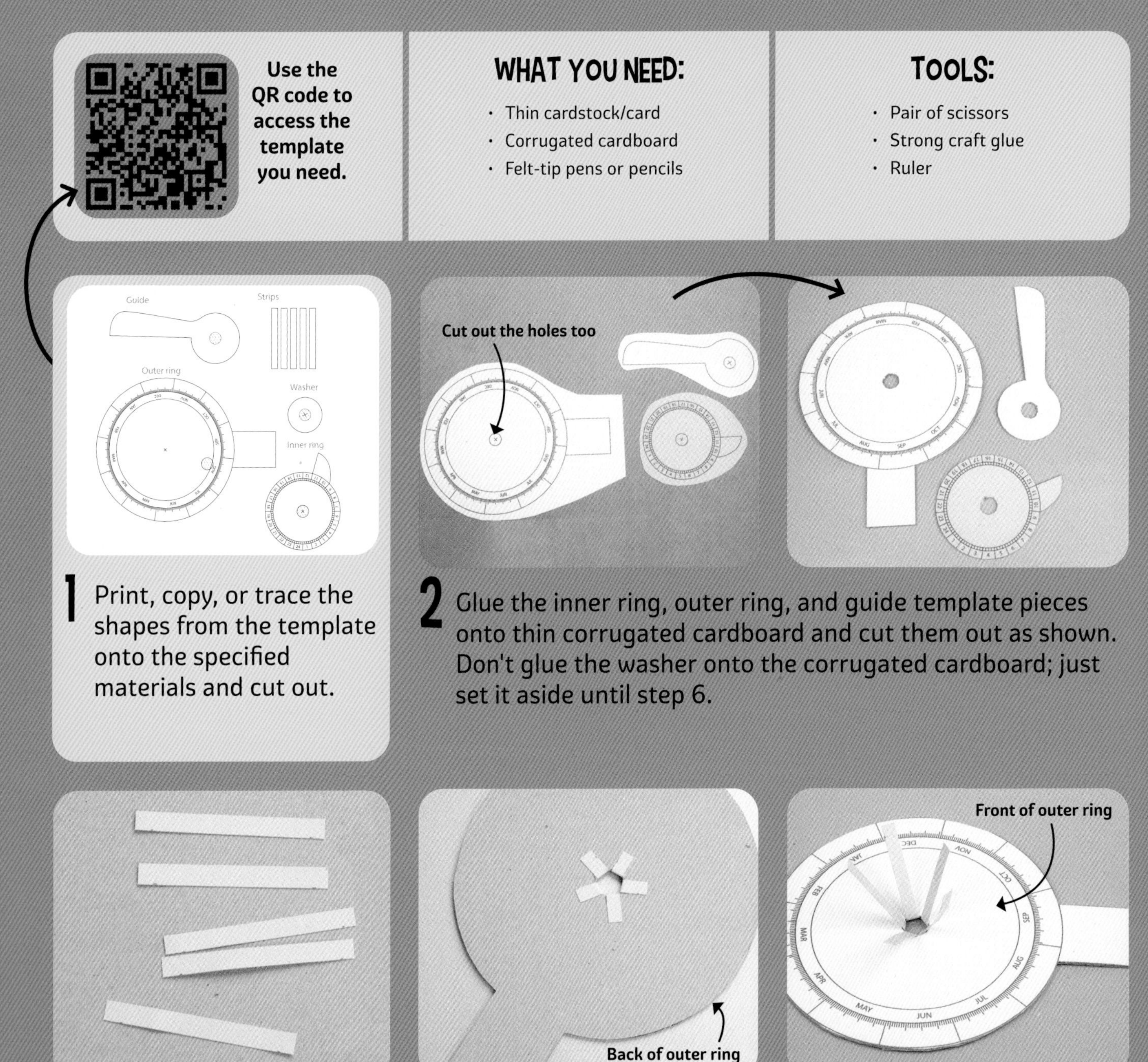

Use the QR code to access the template you need.

WHAT YOU NEED:

- Thin cardstock/card
- Corrugated cardboard
- Felt-tip pens or pencils

TOOLS:

- Pair of scissors
- Strong craft glue
- Ruler

1 Print, copy, or trace the shapes from the template onto the specified materials and cut out.

2 Glue the inner ring, outer ring, and guide template pieces onto thin corrugated cardboard and cut them out as shown. Don't glue the washer onto the corrugated cardboard; just set it aside until step 6.

3 Fill in both sides of the five strips of cardstock/card with felt-tip pens or pencils, per template instructions.

4 Thread the strips through the hole in the outer ring. Glue ½ inch (12mm) of each to the back as shown.

5 Flip the model over, straightening the long strips upward as shown.

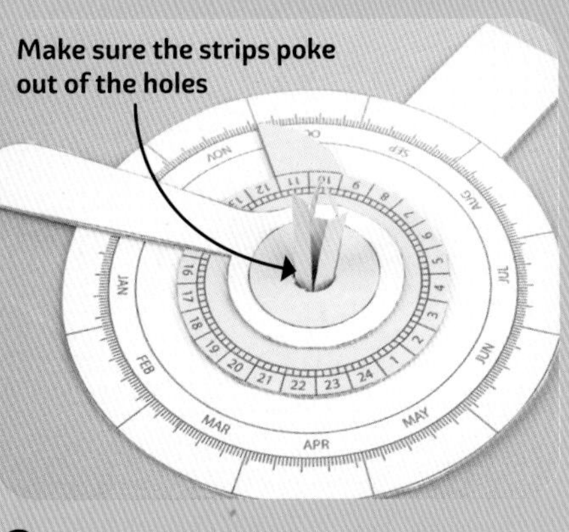

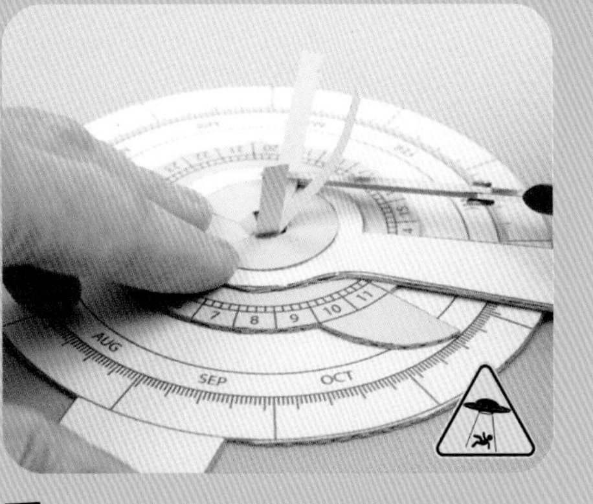

6 Thread the inner ring, guide, and washer on top of the outer ring in that order.

7 Fold the strips down and cut off any excess so they aren't longer than the washer. Glue them down.

TOP TIP

Once assembled, you should be able to twist each piece of the nocturnal indepedently.

How to use your nocturnal:

1. Turn the inner ring so that the finger is pointing toward the current date.

2. Hold the nocturnal upright and sight the North Star through the middle hole.

3. Rotate the guide to line up the flat edge with the two edge stars of Ursa Major. Read the time from the inner ring.

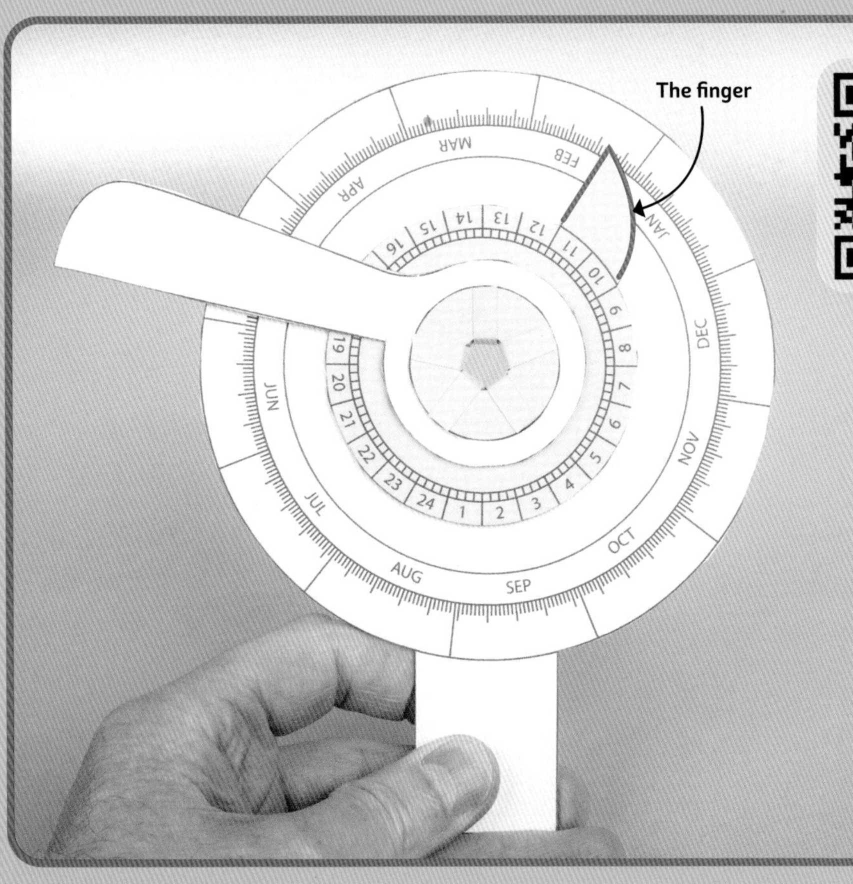

SCAN TO SEE HOW TO USE THE NOCTURNAL!

CONSTELLATIONS

Make these pocket-size constellations to help you learn and identify the beautiful stars in the sky.

Use the QR code to access the template you need.

WHAT YOU NEED:

- Poster tube 3 inches (80mm) in diameter
- Plain paper
- Black cardstock/card
- Corrugated cardboard
- Flashlight/torch or mini battery-operated lights

TOOLS:

- Pair of scissors
- Strong craft glue
- Embroidery needle or push pin

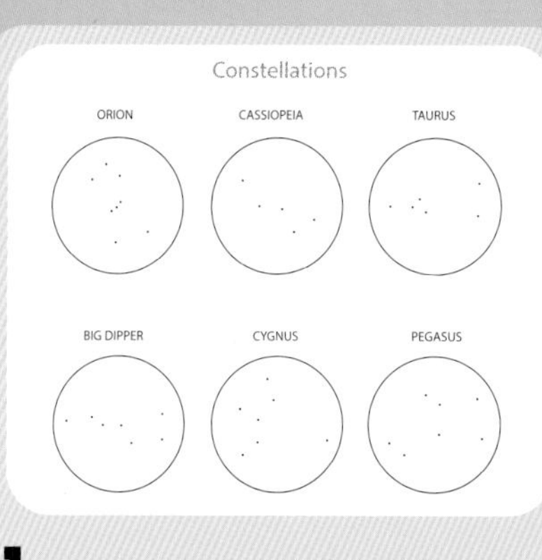

1 Print, copy, or trace the shapes from the template onto plain paper and cut out. Choose one constellation to start with.

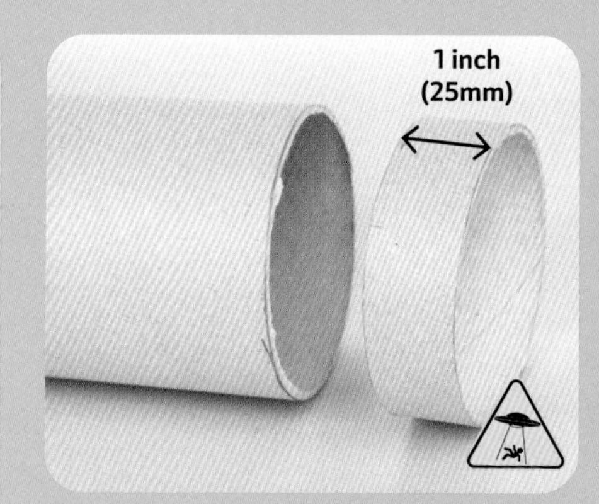

2 Ask an adult to cut a 1 inch (25mm) wide ring out of a poster tube (see page 10). Don't have a poster tube? Use an empty tape roll.

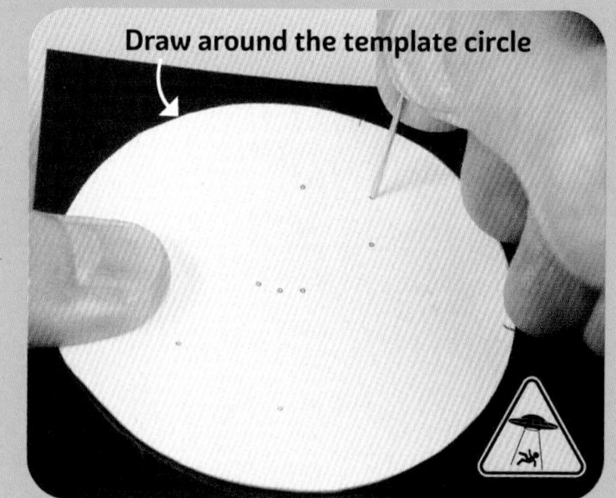

3 Hold the constellation over black cardstock/card. Pierce the stars with a needle or push pin so the holes go through both layers.

4 Cut out the black cardstock/card constellation circle.

5 Glue the constellation circle to the end of the poster tube ring and glue the name to the side of the tube. Why not decorate it, too!

6 When you're outside stargazing, shine your flashlight/torch through the back of the tube to help you identify constellations.

Place some battery-operated lights inside and turn on to view the constellations whenever you like!

Try this craft with all the constellations provided!

LOOK FOR THE CONSTELLATIONS ON A CLEAR AND STARRY NIGHT!

DID YOU KNOW?

If you looked at the sky every night, you would notice that the constellations change throughout the year. This is because the Earth is constantly moving around the Sun, whereas the faraway stars are not.

EQUATORIAL SUNDIAL

Sundials were used to tell the time long before clocks were invented. They use the Sun's shadow to show the time throughout the day.

Use the QR code to access the template you need.

WHAT YOU NEED:

- Poster tube 3 inches (80mm) in diameter
- Thin white cardstock/card
- Bamboo skewer
- 2 pieces of corrugated cardboard

TOOLS:

- Pencil
- Ruler
- Strong craft glue
- Pair of scissors
- Semi-circular (180 degree) protractor

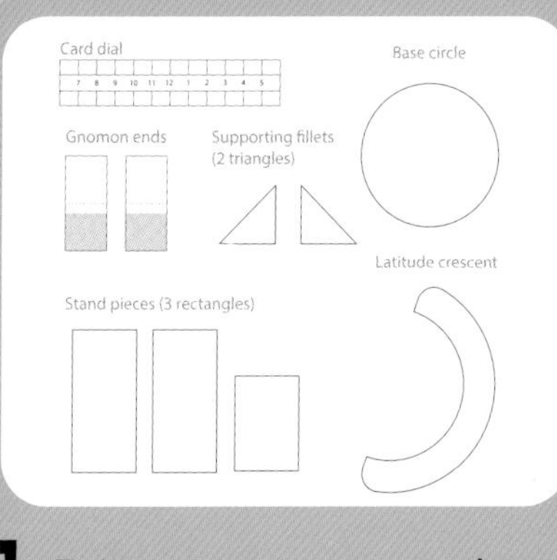

1 Print, copy, or trace the shapes from the template onto the specified materials and cut out.

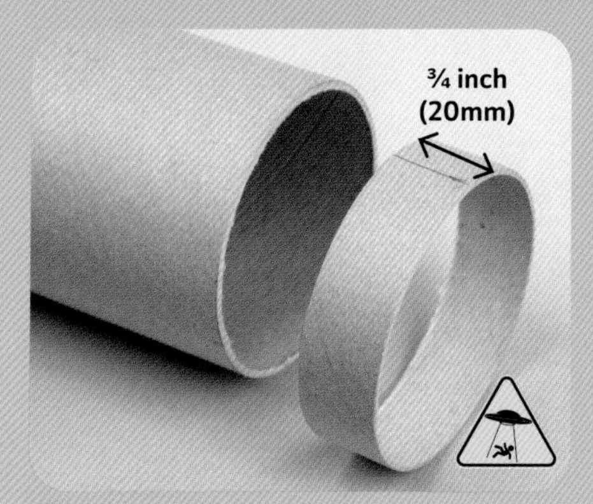

2 Ask an adult to cut a ¾ inch (20mm) wide ring out of a poster tube (see page 10).

TOP TIP

If you don't have a poster tube, you could use an empty tape roll!

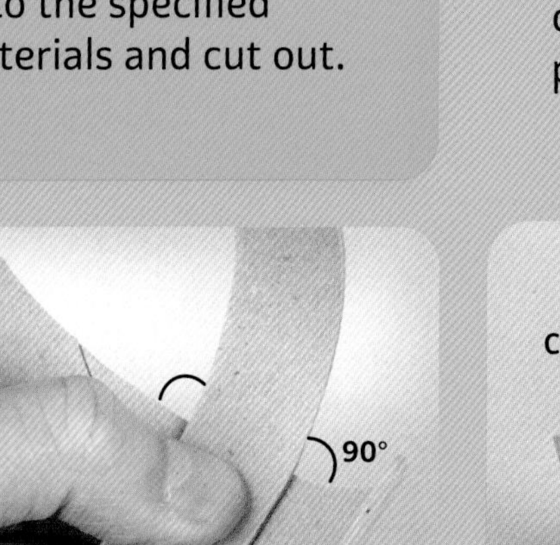

3 Cut the poster tube ring in half to make two semi-circles. Then, glue the two together at a 90-degree angle as shown.

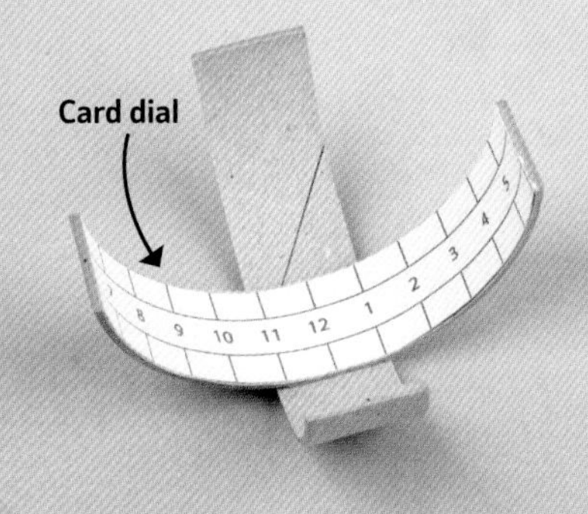

4 Glue the card dial to the top tube as shown, then set aside until step 7.

This is a gnomon end. Gnomon is pronounced "no-mon".

5 Take one of the gnomon end rectangles and glue two corners together as shown. Repeat for the second gnomon end.

Trim the skewer to fit snugly in the half tube

Glue here

6 Once dry, thread a trimmed skewer into the gnomon ends as shown. Glue in place.

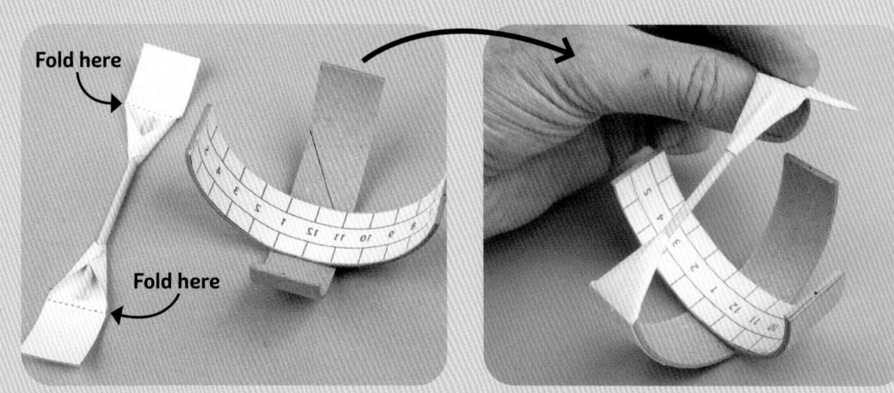

7 Fold inward along the dotted lines. Re-open and apply glue to the surface, then turn over the gnomon and attach each end to the tube without the dial. Set aside until step 11.

8 Sandwich the small stand piece between the two bigger pieces. Line up the bottoms and glue together to make the stand.

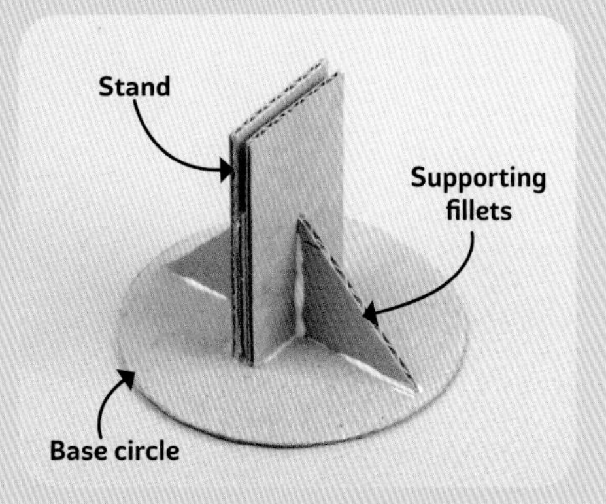

9 Hold the stand upright in the middle of the base circle. Place the supporting fillets on each side of the stand and glue in place.

KEY WORD

LATITUDE

The line around the middle of the Earth is called the equator. Imagine a line wrapped around the Earth where you are. The angle between this line and the equator is your latitude. You can find your latitude with a quick search online.

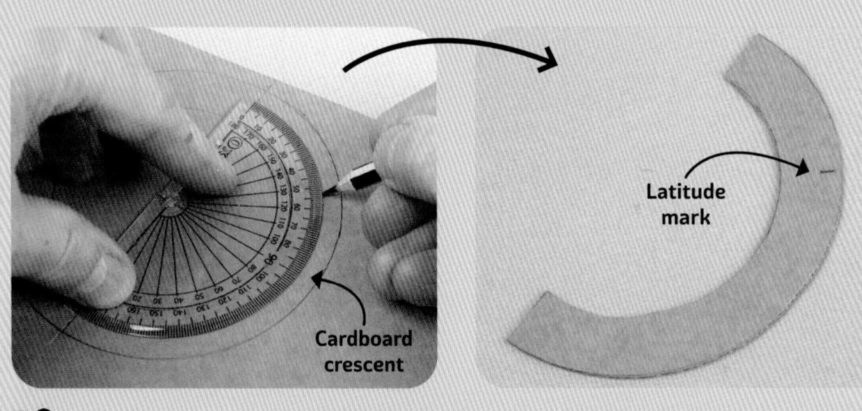

10 Find out the latitude of the place you live and mark that angle on the cardboard crescent from the template, with the aid of a protractor.

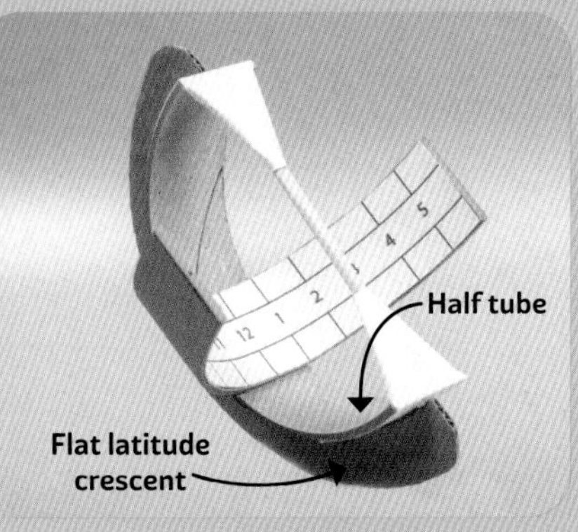

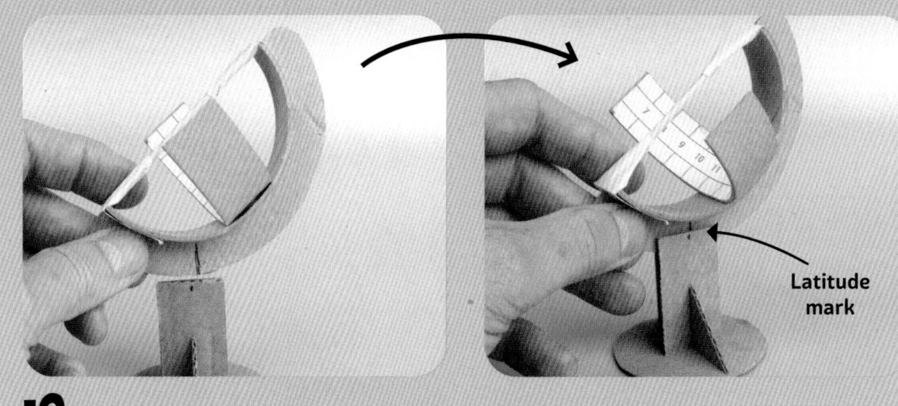

11 Glue the flat latitude crescent to the back of the back half tube as shown.

12 Once everything is dry, fit the sundial into the stand. Make sure that the latitude semi-circle is vertical and the latitude mark is fitted into the middle of the stand. Glue in place.

How to use your equatorial sundial:

1. Line up the sundial so that the gnomon faces north.

2. Read the time when the Sun shines by seeing where the shadow is cast on the dial.

3. If it's Daylight Saving Time, you may need to add or subtract an hour from your reading!

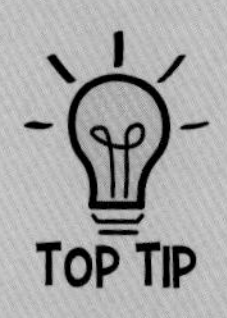

TOP TIP

Use a compass, or the North Star, Polaris, to find North.

USE YOUR SUNDIAL TO TELL THE TIME!

DID YOU KNOW?

The oldest sundial ever discovered dates to 1500 BCE. However, it's thought that as far back as 3500 BCE, people told the time by wedging a stick in the ground and watching the length of the shadow change. Sundials are much more decorative now, like this one here.

AWESOME MODEL SPACECRAFT

Humans have been curious about outer space for centuries, but it wasn't until the 1950s that the first spacecraft went beyond Earth's atmosphere.

PREPARING FOR LIFTOFF

Spacecraft, like rockets, need to be strong and super fast to escape the pull of Earth's **gravity.** Because everything is so far away in space travel, spacecraft also need to carry lots of heavy fuel. This can make flying more difficult.

SPACECRAFT EXPLORATION

Scientists have learned more about outer space by sending clever robotic machines to explore where humans haven't yet been. Rovers on Mars are controlled by **NASA**'s scientists on Earth. It takes about 7 months to get them there, and not all rovers have landed safely!

WANT TO KNOW MORE?

This chapter allows you to make your very own model spacecraft. They may be smaller than real-life rockets, shuttles, and planet-exploring machines, but they can still fly, hover, and zoom!

STOMP ROCKET

5... 4... 3... 2... 1... LIFTOFF!
How high can you catapult your rocket with this out-of-this-world project?

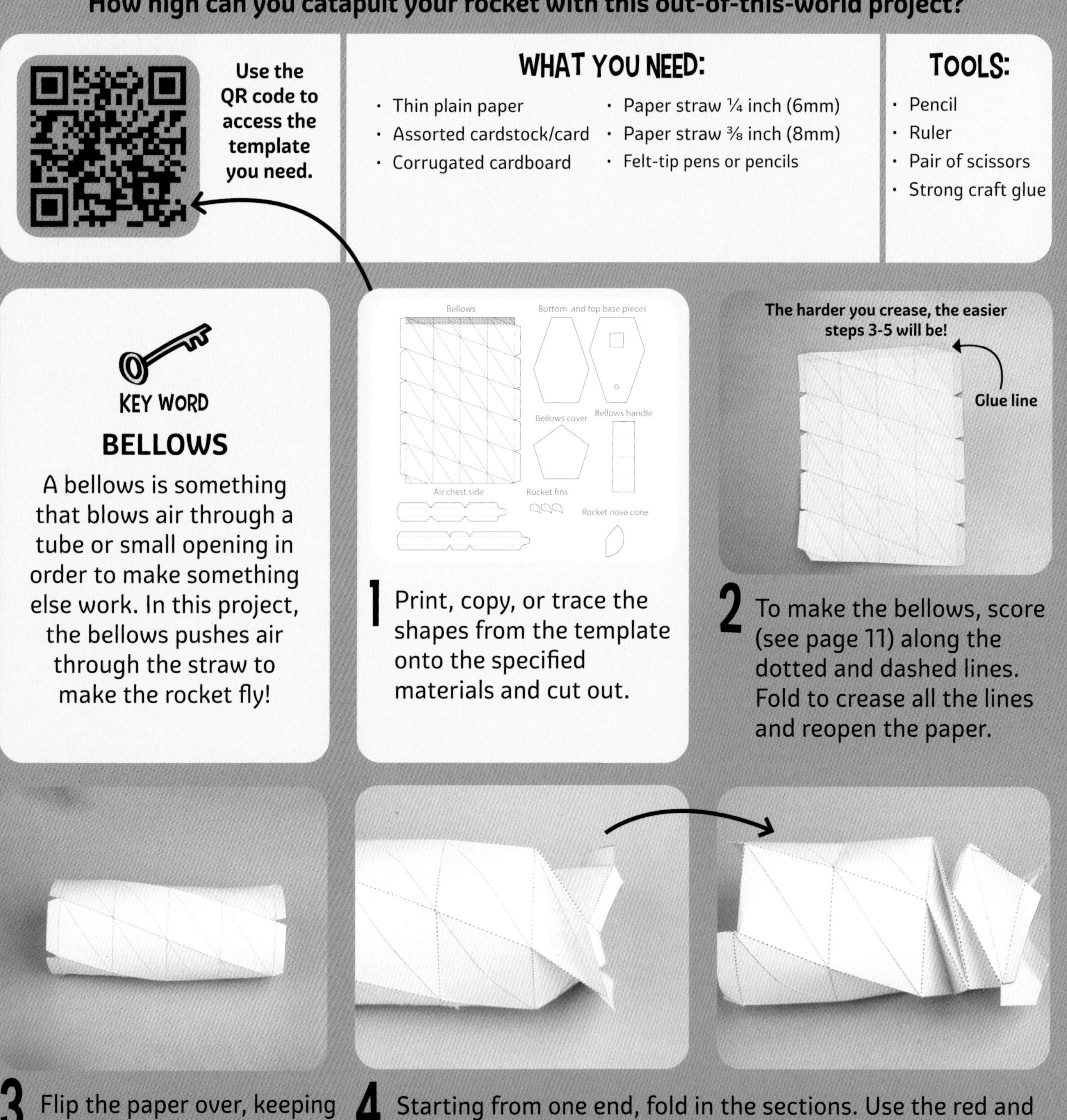

Use the QR code to access the template you need.

WHAT YOU NEED:

- Thin plain paper
- Assorted cardstock/card
- Corrugated cardboard
- Paper straw ¼ inch (6mm)
- Paper straw ⅜ inch (8mm)
- Felt-tip pens or pencils

TOOLS:

- Pencil
- Ruler
- Pair of scissors
- Strong craft glue

KEY WORD

BELLOWS

A bellows is something that blows air through a tube or small opening in order to make something else work. In this project, the bellows pushes air through the straw to make the rocket fly!

1 Print, copy, or trace the shapes from the template onto the specified materials and cut out.

2 To make the bellows, score (see page 11) along the dotted and dashed lines. Fold to crease all the lines and reopen the paper.

3 Flip the paper over, keeping the glue line at the top. Roll up from the bottom to make a tube. Line up the edges carefully, then glue along the glue line.

4 Starting from one end, fold in the sections. Use the red and green codes on the template to help guide you. Fold down on the green dotted lines (valley folds) and fold up on the red dashed lines (hill folds). **Scan the QR code above to watch how to fold the bellows.**

5 Work your way down the tube, folding one section at a time. The completed bellows should look like the image above.

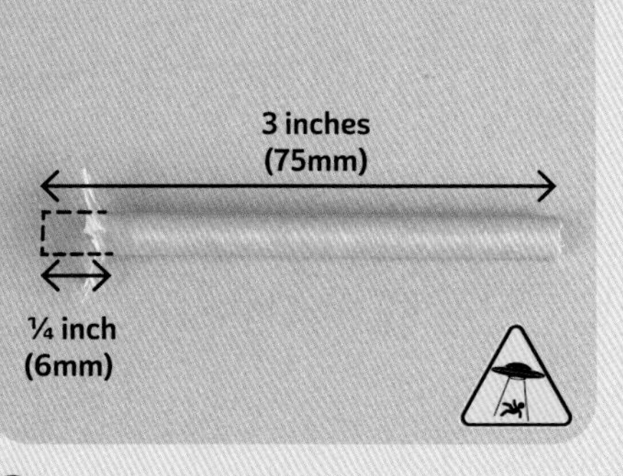

6 Cut the thin straw to 3 inches (75mm). Cut glue strips at one end of the straw ¼ inch (6mm) deep and bend outward.

7 Thread the straw into the circular hole in the top base piece as shown. Glue the strips to stick them to the underneath.

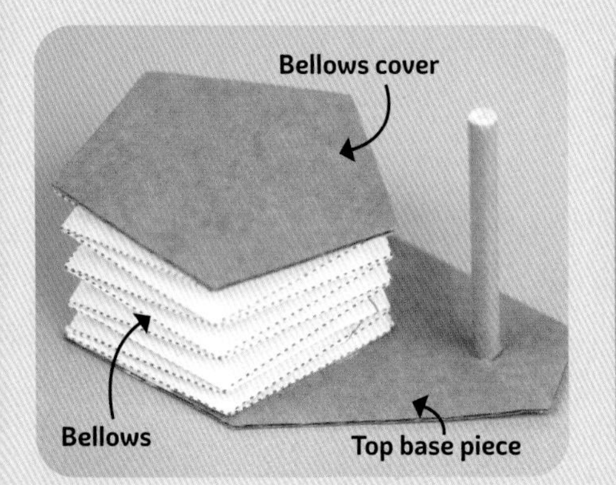

8 Glue the bellows to the top of the top base piece, lining up the bottom edge. Then, glue the bellows cover from the template on top.

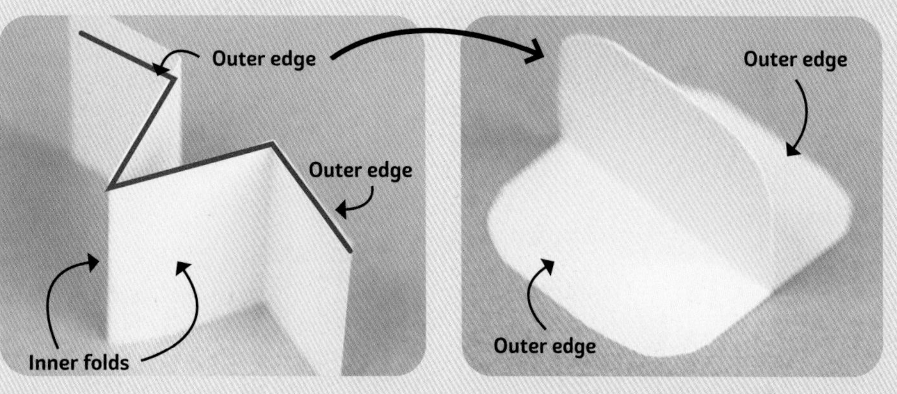

9 Take the bellows handle from the template. Fold along the dotted and dashes lines to crease the zigzag shape shown. Glue the inner folds together, leaving the outer edges folded outward. Cut the corners to make them rounded as shown.

10 Glue the handle to the top of the bellows cover. Then, set aside until step 12.

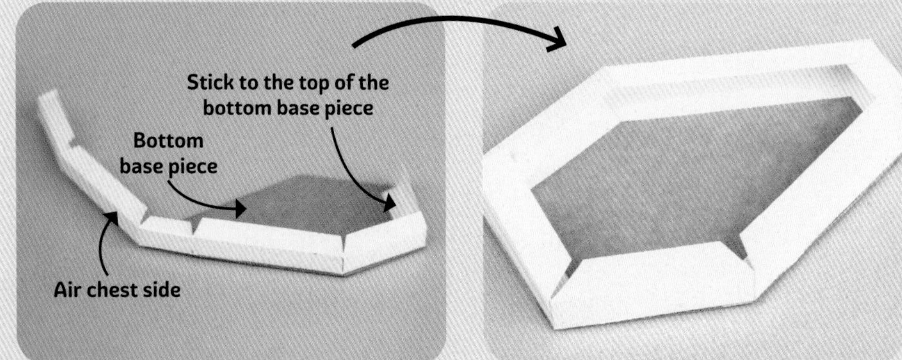

11 Using the letter guides on the template, wrap and glue the air chest side pieces around the bottom base piece. It should fit all the way around and look like the photo above.

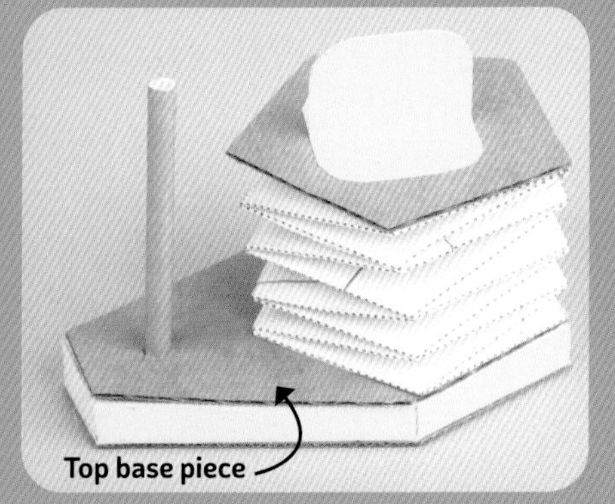

12 Apply glue to the top of the air chest side, line up the top base piece on top and press down to glue together.

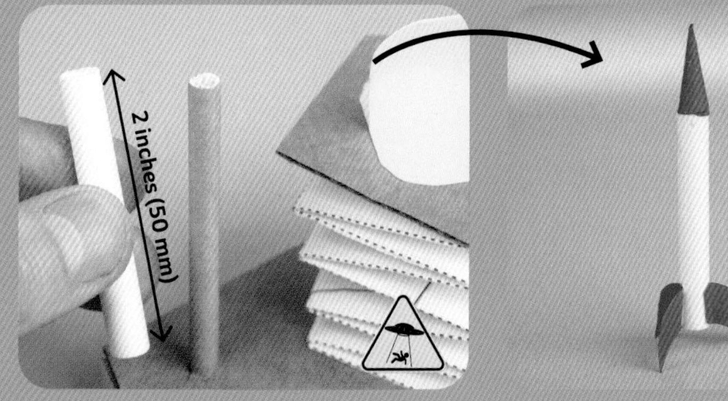

13 To make your rocket, cut the wider straw to 2 inches (50mm) in length so it's slightly shorter than the straw in the top base piece. Add a paper cone to the top and fins to the bottom to decorate the rocket.

DID YOU KNOW?

Rockets must travel faster than 7 miles (11km) per second to escape Earth's gravity – the force pulling them back to the ground. This speed is called escape velocity. It takes lots of fuel and power to travel that fast!

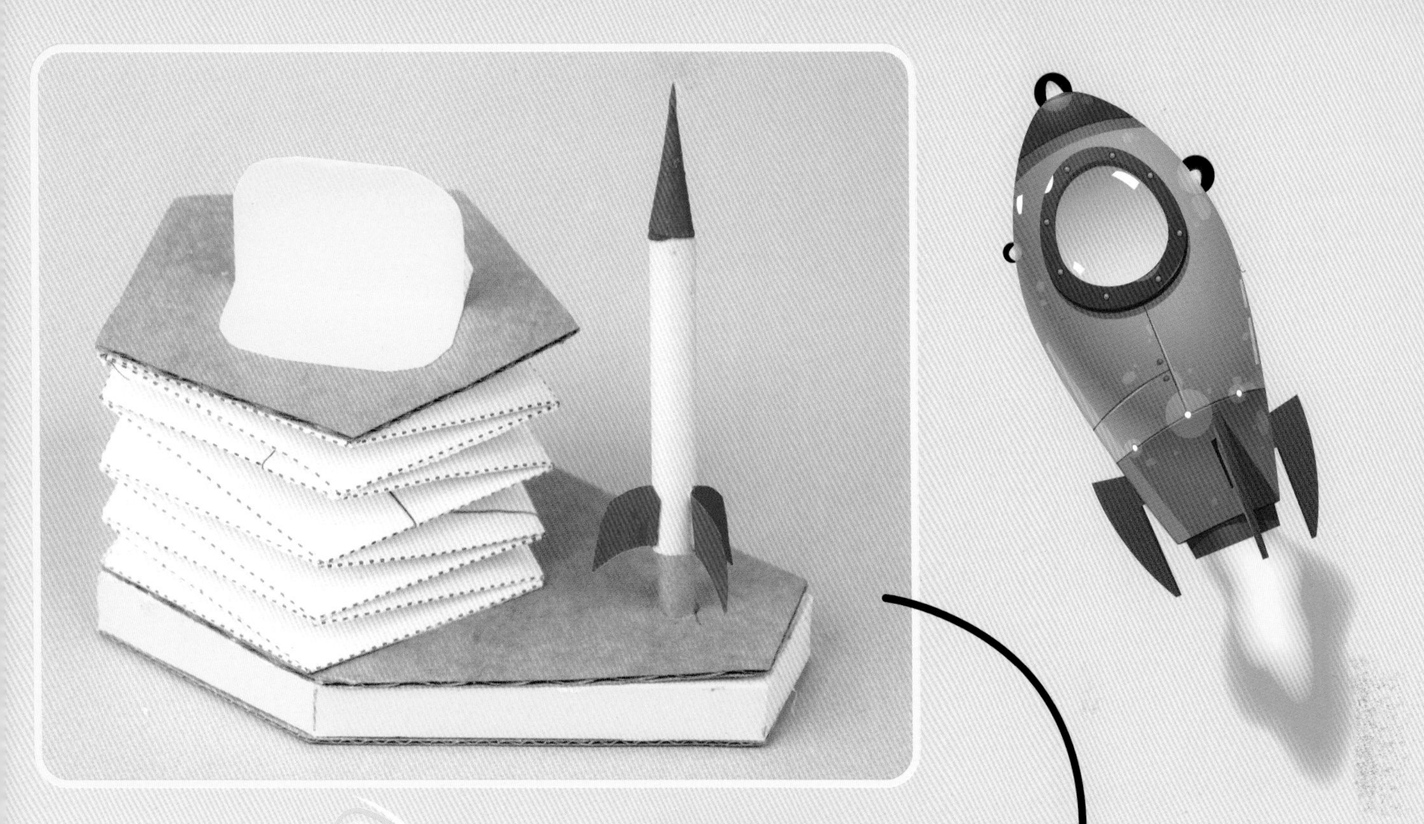

PRESS DOWN THE BELLOWS SHARPLY TO LAUNCH THE ROCKET INTO SPACE!

MOON LANDER

Make a simple Moon lander model with this curious craft. What do you think it's like to land on the Moon?

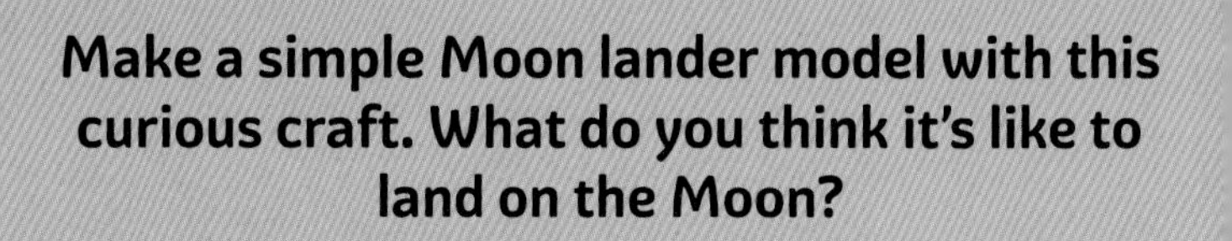

WHAT YOU NEED:

- Electrical connector block
- Long paper fasteners/split pins

TOOLS:

- Strong craft glue
- Needle pliers
- Screwdriver

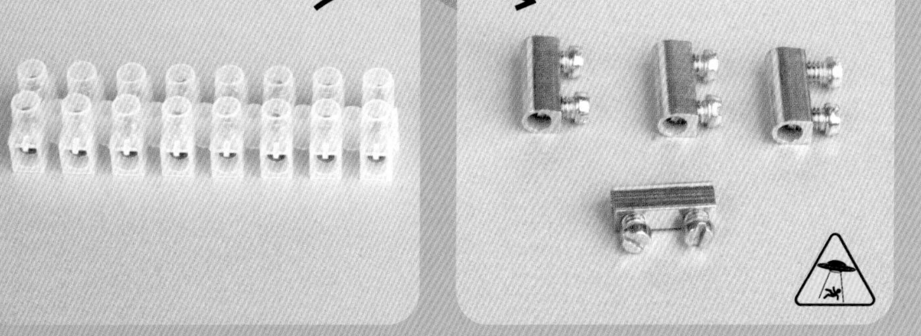

1 Carefully cut out four of the brass sections from the electrical connector block strip.

2 Glue the four connector blocks together with strong craft glue to make the body of the lander as shown.

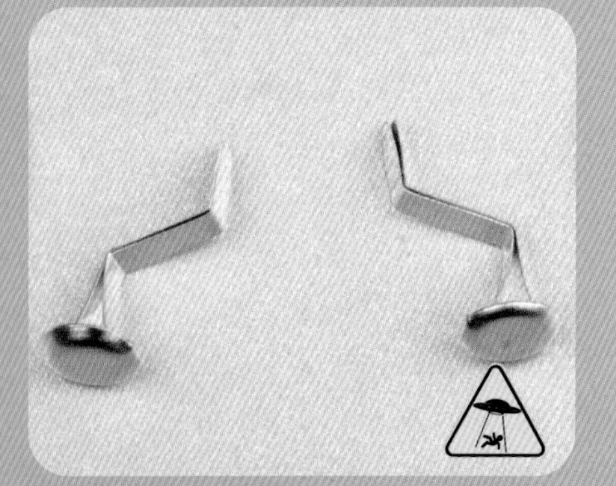

3 Ask an adult to bend angles into the paper fasteners/split pins to make four legs.

4 Thread the legs into the brass blocks. Tighten the screws with a screwdriver to secure the legs in place.

CREATE A SPACE SCENE FOR YOUR AWESOME MOON LANDER!

DID YOU KNOW?

There's no wind on the Moon, which means that the first astronauts' footsteps are probably still there!

ROCKET CAROUSEL

Make a fantastic fairground carousel featuring rocket rides!

Use the QR code to access the template you need.

WHAT YOU NEED:

- Assorted cardstock/card
- Corrugated cardboard
- Wooden skewer, cut to 3 inches (75mm)

TOOLS:

- Pencil
- Pair of scissors
- Strong craft glue

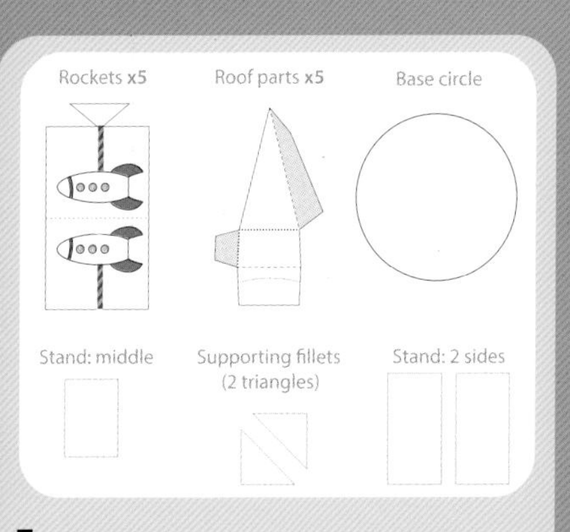

1 Print, copy, or trace the shapes from the template onto the specified materials and cut out.

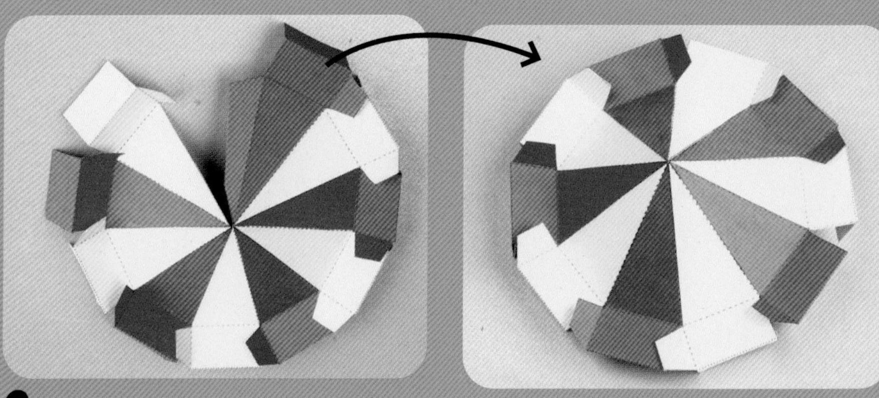

2 Crease and score (see page 11) along the fold lines of the roof parts from the template. Using alternating pieces, glue the main triangle sections together using the glue flaps as shown. Fitting in the final piece will make a shallow cone shape.

Cut along the curved line to create a scalloped effect

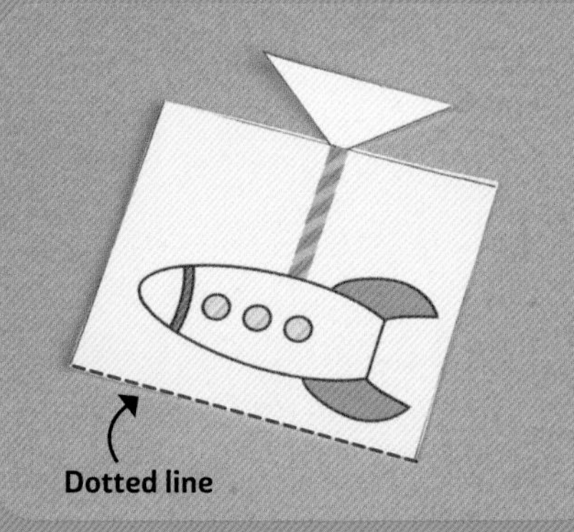

Dotted line

3 Fold up the outer edges to make them vertical. Then, layer and glue the outer edge pieces together using the glue tabs. Fold backward along the straight line of each outer piece and glue down to hide the glue tabs.

4 For the rockets, fold along the dotted line so that the pictures show on each side. They need to perfectly line up so they're double-sided once cut out.

5 Unfold, apply glue to the paper, and refold. Allow it to dry, then carefully cut out the rocket as shown. Repeat for all five rockets.

6 Turn the roof upside down, then glue the triangle section above the rockets to alternate sections of the roof.

7 To make the stand, place the smaller cardboard piece between the two bigger pieces. Line up the bottoms and glue together.

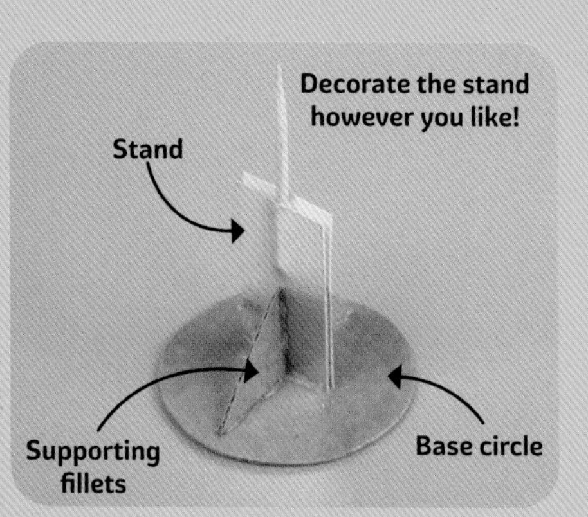

8 Glue the stand upright in the middle of the base circle, followed by one supporting fillet on each side. Glue and slide the skewer into the middle.

Balance your carousel roof on the point of the skewer

GIVE YOUR CAROUSEL A PUSH TO SET THE ROCKETS SPINNING!

MARS ROVER

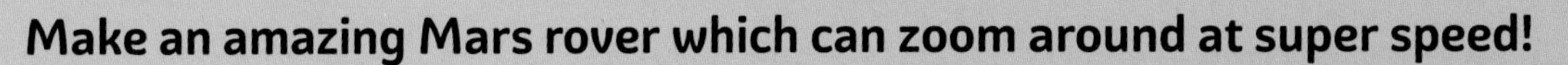

Make an amazing Mars rover which can zoom around at super speed!

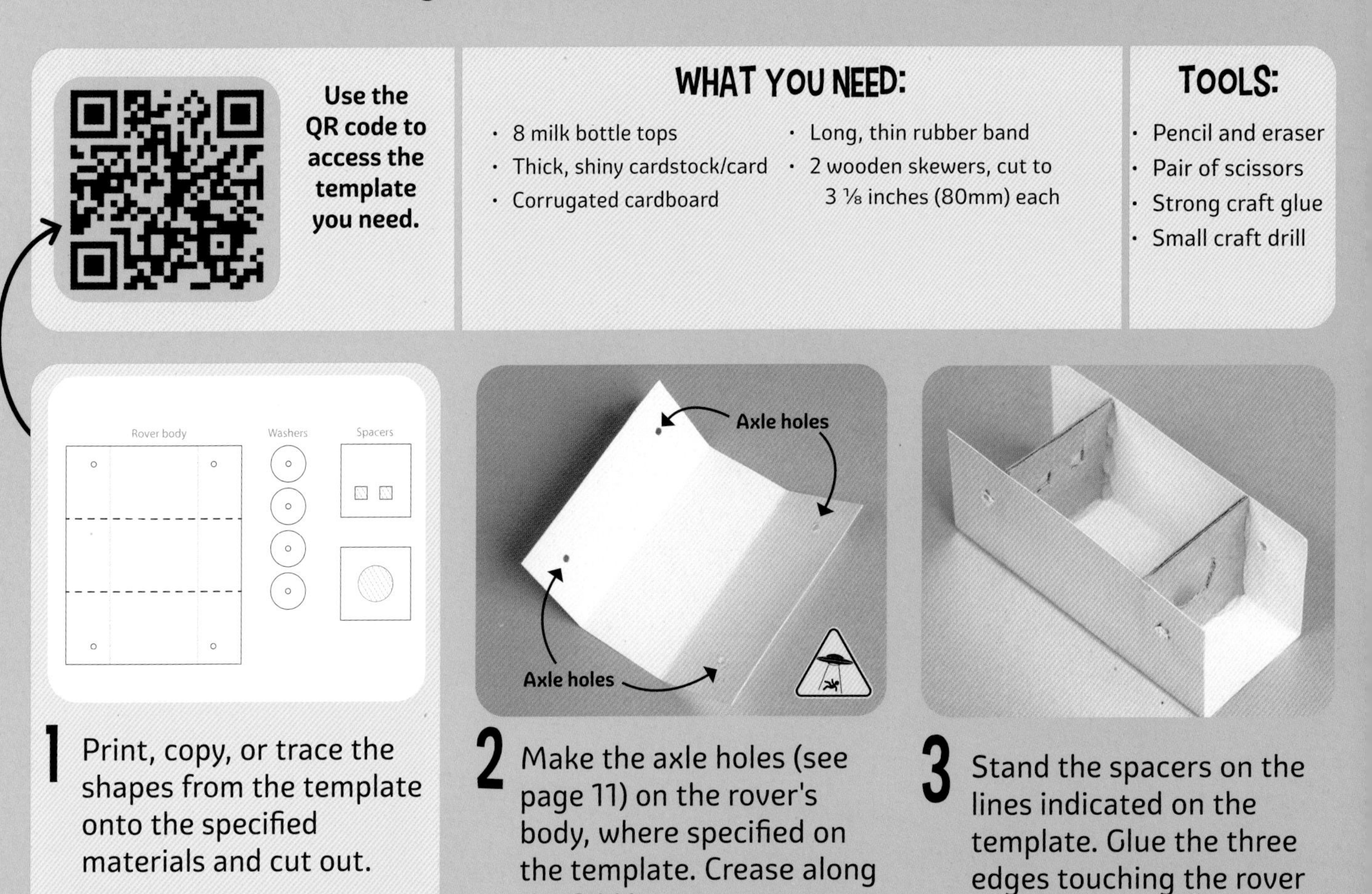

Use the QR code to access the template you need.

WHAT YOU NEED:

- 8 milk bottle tops
- Thick, shiny cardstock/card
- Corrugated cardboard
- Long, thin rubber band
- 2 wooden skewers, cut to 3 ⅛ inches (80mm) each

TOOLS:

- Pencil and eraser
- Pair of scissors
- Strong craft glue
- Small craft drill

1 Print, copy, or trace the shapes from the template onto the specified materials and cut out.

2 Make the axle holes (see page 11) on the rover's body, where specified on the template. Crease along the fold lines.

3 Stand the spacers on the lines indicated on the template. Glue the three edges touching the rover body to secure them.

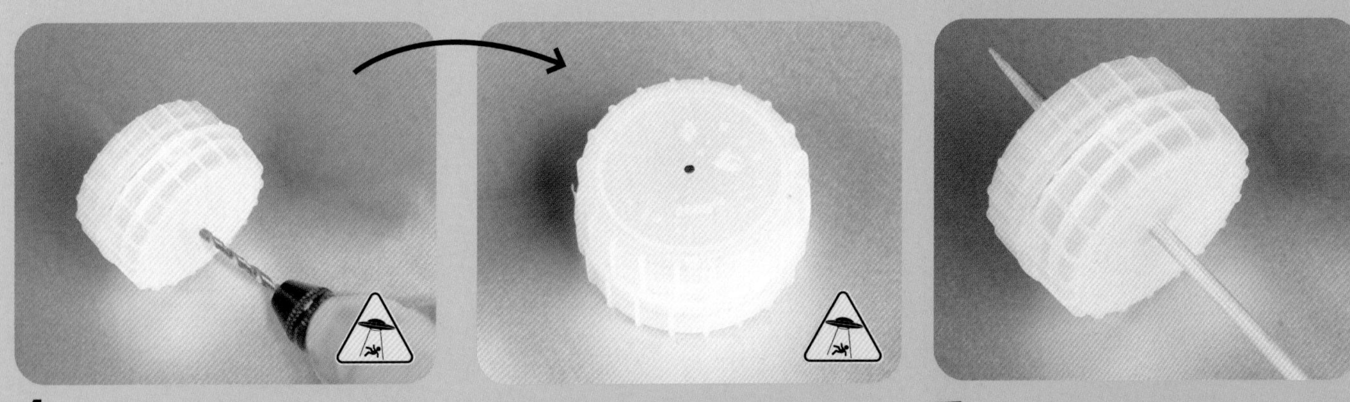

4 Ask an adult to make holes in the middle of each milk bottle top using a small craft drill. The holes must be precise for the craft to work. Test the holes are lined up by threading a skewer through. Once happy, split the tops into pairs, gluing each pair together along their bottom edges.

5 Once dry, thread a wooden skewer through one wheel and glue around the holes to attach.

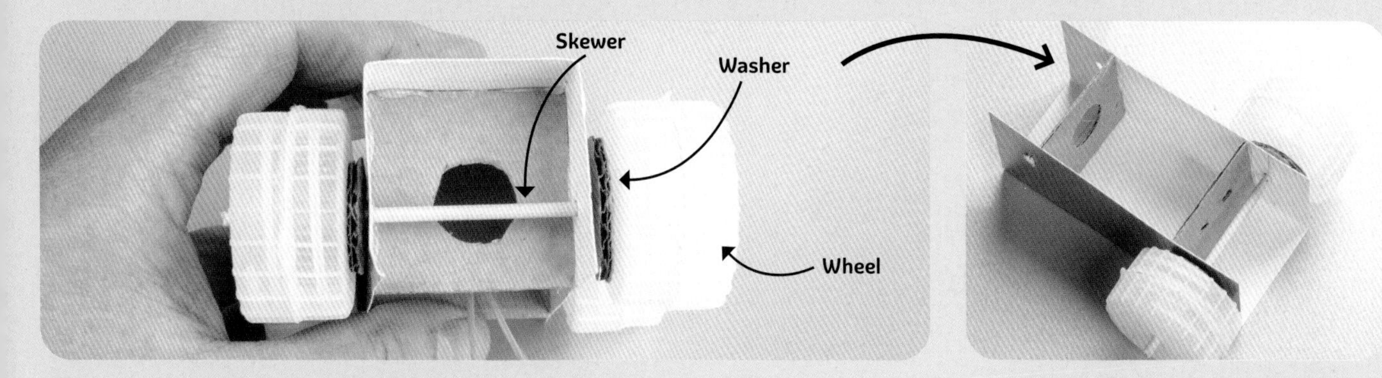

6 Thread a cardboard washer onto the skewer, pushing it up to the wheel. Thread the skewer through a pair of axle holes, sandwiching the washer between the wheel and the rover body. Slide a washer and wheel onto the other side of the skewer. Trim the skewer, leaving a little at each side, and glue the wheel in place. Repeat for the second set of wheels.

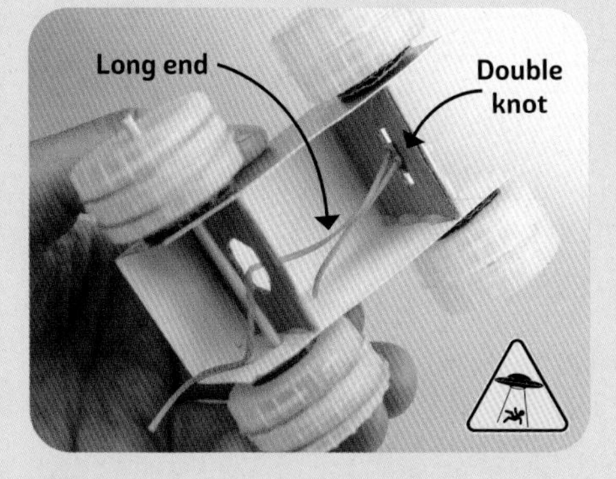

7 Cut a rubber band to make a single length. Tie it in a double knot through the double-holed spacer, leaving one side very long.

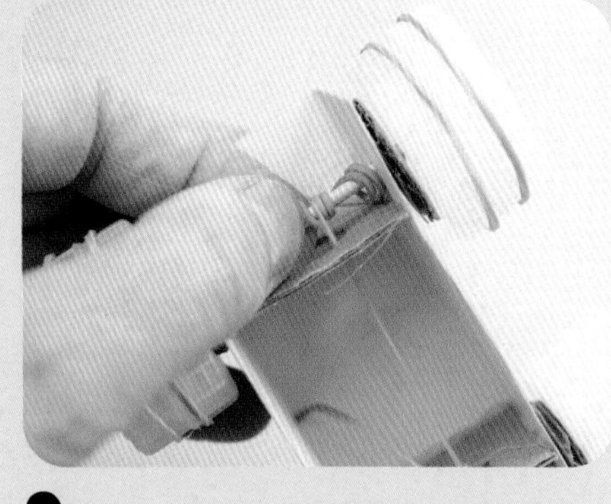

8 To use the rover, wrap the long end of the rubber band around the opposite skewer and wind up until tight. Place the rover on a flat surface, then release!

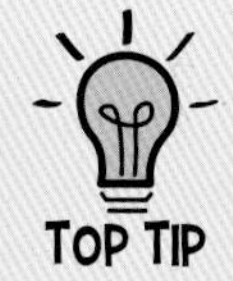

TOP TIP

If you get too much wheel spin, you can increase the grip by adding short rubber bands around the wheels (see steps 7 and 8).

WATCH THE THE ROVER DASH ALONG!

BLOWPIPE SPACE SHUTTLE

Launch your very own space shuttle with this quick, cool craft!

Use the QR code to access the template you need.

WHAT YOU NEED:

- Paper straw ¼ inch (6mm)
- Paper straw ⅜ inch (8mm)
- Adhesive/sticky putty
- Plain paper

TOOLS:

- Pair of scissors
- Strong craft glue
- Ruler

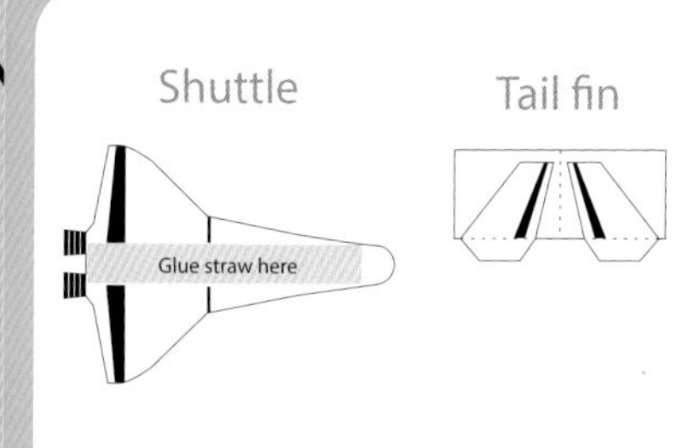

1 Print, copy, or trace the shapes from the template onto plain paper and cut out.

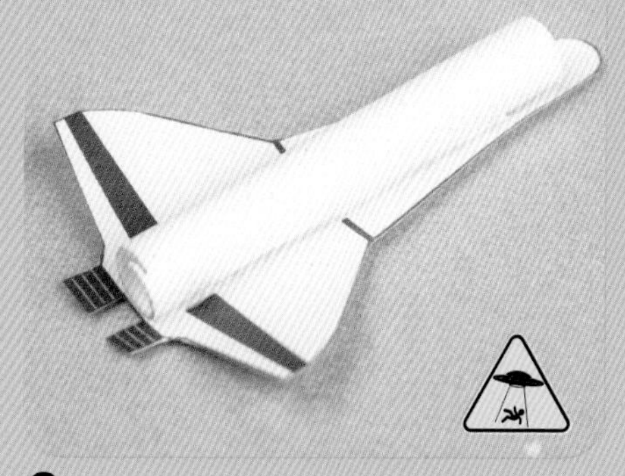

2 Cut the ⅜ inch (8mm) wide straw to 2 $\frac{3}{16}$ inch (55mm) long. Place the straw on top of the shuttle and glue in place.

3 Fold the wings up slightly as shown. The angle of the wings is called dihedral. It helps with stability in flight.

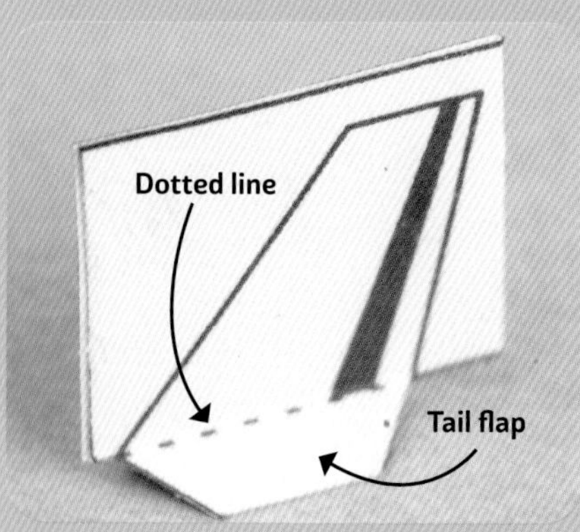

4 Fold the tail fin piece in half along the dotted line. Glue these two sides together, but don't glue the tail flaps.

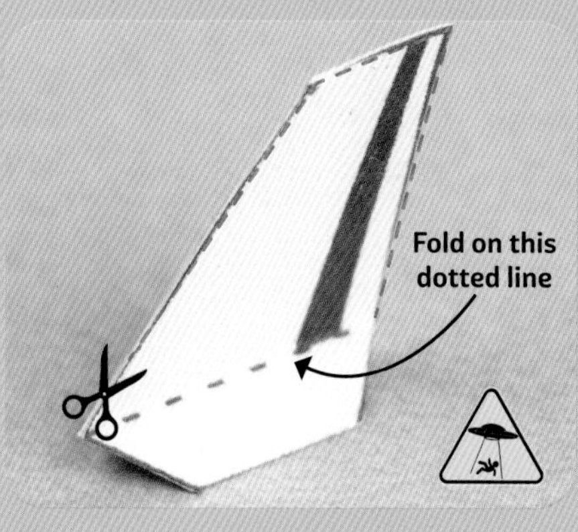

5 Cut around the tail fin as shown. Fold along the dotted lines of the tail flaps and open them outward.

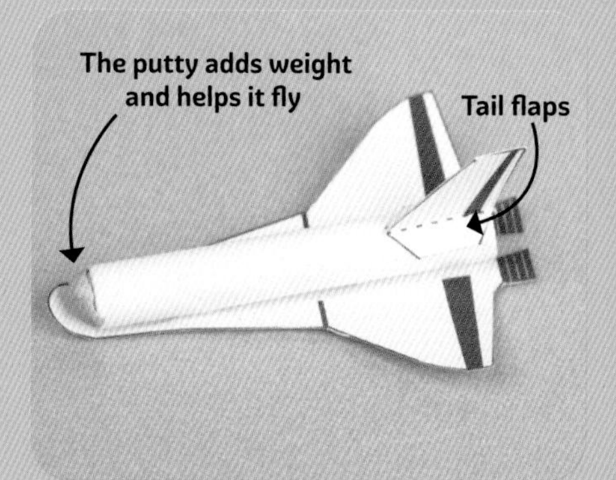

6 Glue the tail flaps to the straw as shown. Place a small piece of adhesive/sticky putty on the other end of the straw.

7 Thread your shuttle onto the ¼ inch (6mm) straw. Launch the shuttle by blowing a sharp breath through the straw.

5... 4... 3... 2... 1... BLAST OFF!

DID YOU KNOW?

The space shuttle was the first spacecraft that could be used again and again. Each time a space shuttle was launched, it was called a mission. The space shuttle went on 135 missions in total!

ORIGAMI MARS LANDER

TOP TIP

Origami is a lot easier to follow when watching a video! Scan the QR code to watch how to make it.

Origami, the Japanese art of folding paper into decorative shapes and figures, is a fun way to make models!

Use the QR code to see a video of the steps in action.

WHAT YOU NEED:

- Origami paper 6 x 6 inches (150 x 150 mm) square

1 Start with a single square sheet of paper with the diagonals, vertical and horizontal lines creased.

2 Fold from the top right corner to the bottom left. Then, tuck in the other two corners to make a smaller square. Rotate the square 45 degrees so that the open end is at the bottom.

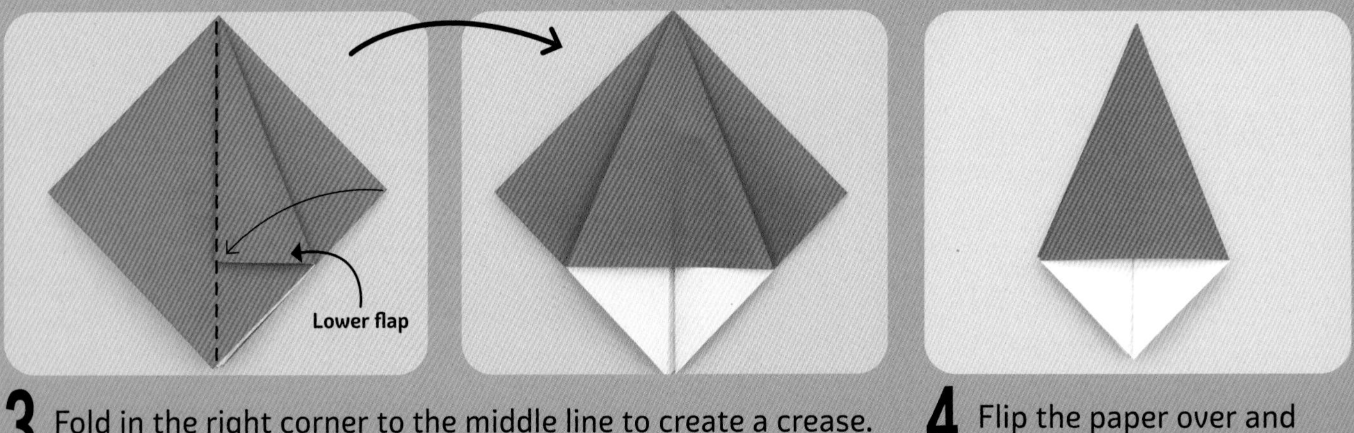

3 Fold in the right corner to the middle line to create a crease. Pull the lower flap out from underneath (by inserting your fingers under the folded area). Open out and flatten the fold by pulling the flap to the bottom left edge to make an inverted kite shape. Crease the paper in place.

4 Flip the paper over and repeat step 3 three more times with the other flaps, like the above image.

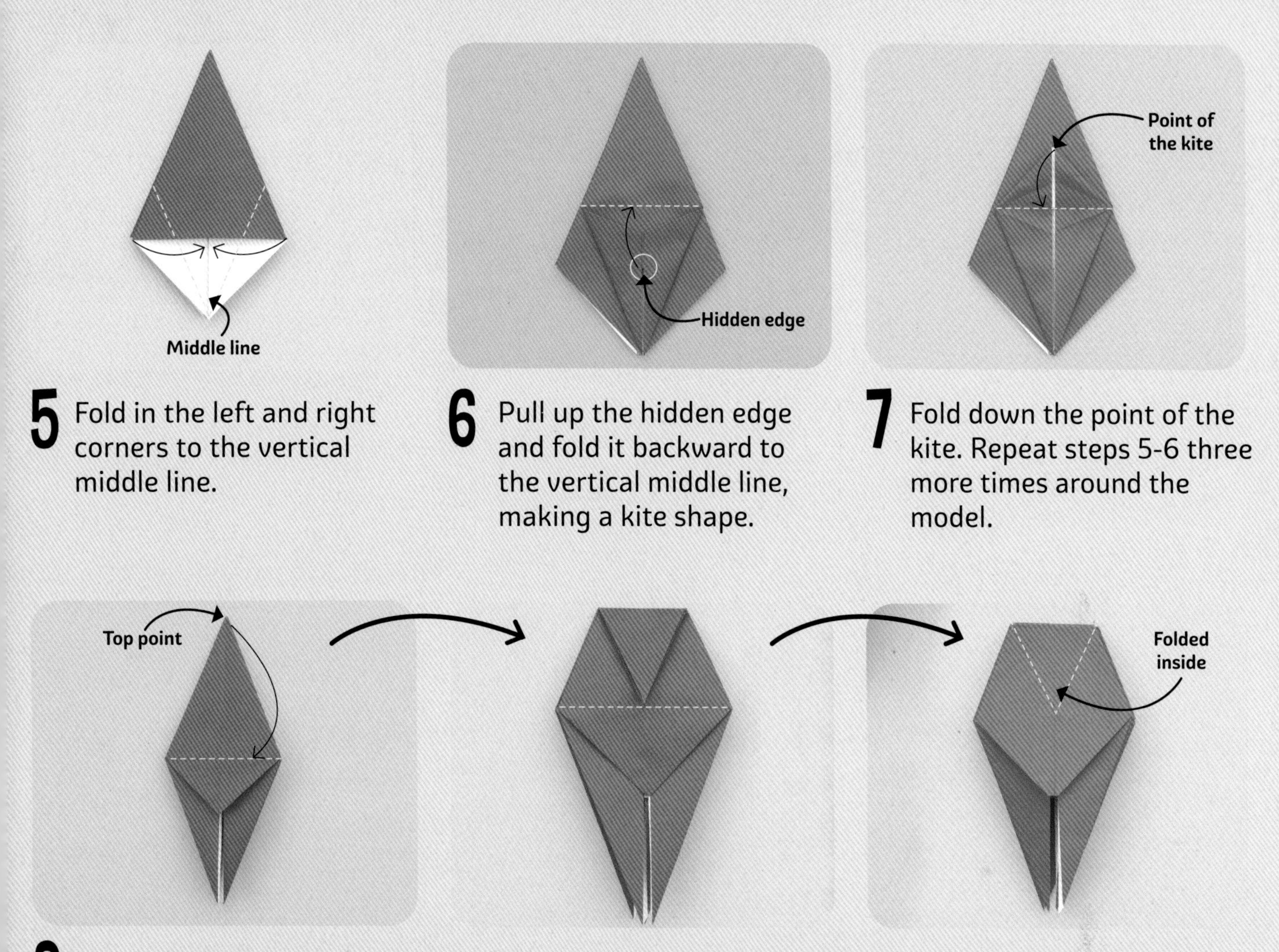

5 Fold in the left and right corners to the vertical middle line.

6 Pull up the hidden edge and fold it backward to the vertical middle line, making a kite shape.

7 Fold down the point of the kite. Repeat steps 5-6 three more times around the model.

8 Fold down the top point to the horizontal line shown and push down to crease. Then, open the fold, flip the model over and repeat on the other side. Loosely open out the model, then push down the newly folded section into the top of the model so that it's tucked inside. Fold the model flat again.

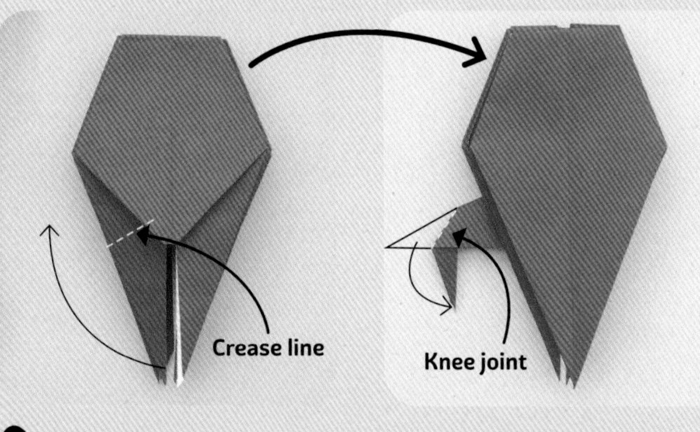

9 Fold up a leg along the crease line as shown. Fold down the knee joint of the leg. Then, repeat this step for the remaining three legs before opening out the model to complete your Mars lander.

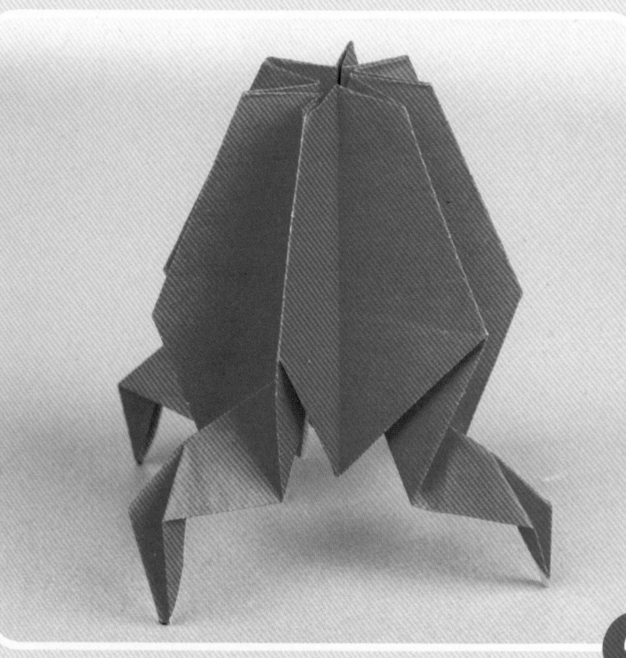

BALANCING UFO

This spaceship hovers mysteriously off the ground. Which faraway planet or galaxy do think it has come from?

Use the QR code to access the template you need.

WHAT YOU NEED:

- Assorted cardstock/card
- Corrugated cardboard circle
- Ping pong/table tennis ball
- Craft cork
- Paper fasteners/ split pins
- Jumbo paper clip
- Bouncy rubber ball 1 inch (25mm)
- Lollipop stick or paper straw

TOOLS:

- Pencil
- Ruler
- Pair of scissors
- Strong craft glue
- Pointy wooden skewer
- Needle pliers
- Sticky tape
- Marker pen

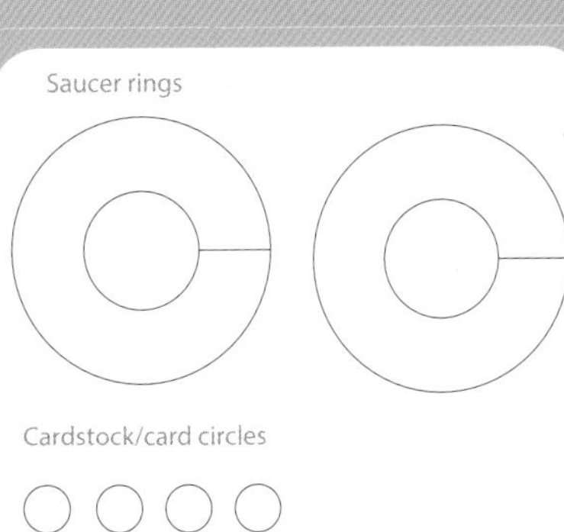

1 Print, copy, or trace the shapes from the template onto the specified materials and cut out.

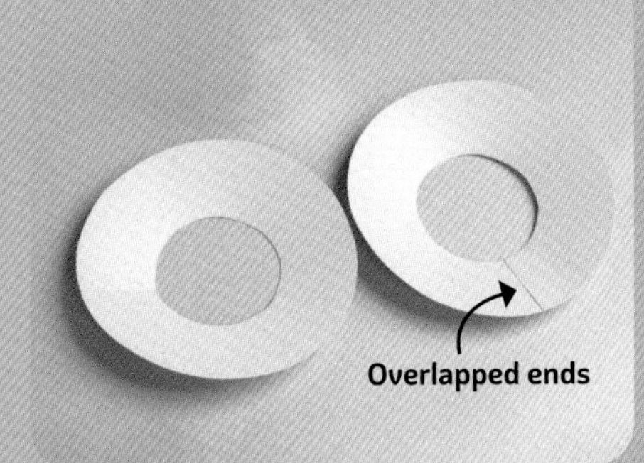

2 Take one saucer ring, overlap the ends, and glue them down. This should create a dome shape. Repeat with the other ring.

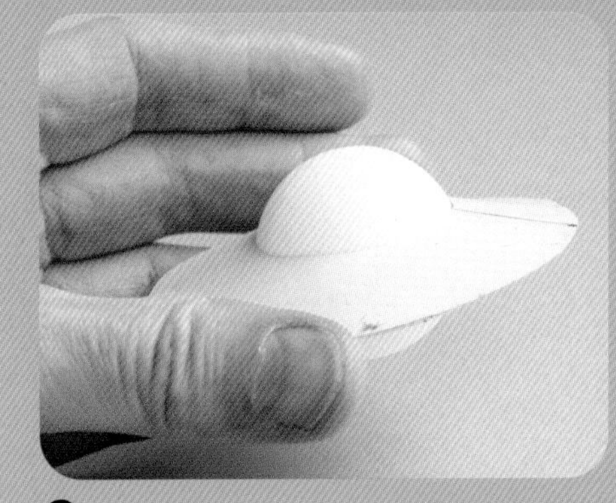

3 Place the rings over the ping pong/table tennis ball with the dome sides facing outward. Glue the edges down to keep the ball secure.

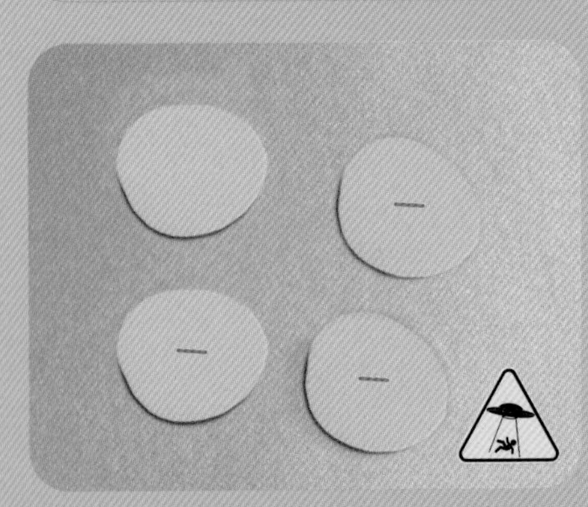

4 To make the legs, cut a small slit in the middle of three of the cardstock/ card circles from the template.

5 Thread a paper fastener/ split pin through the slits and bend the tips in opposite directions. Repeat for the other legs.

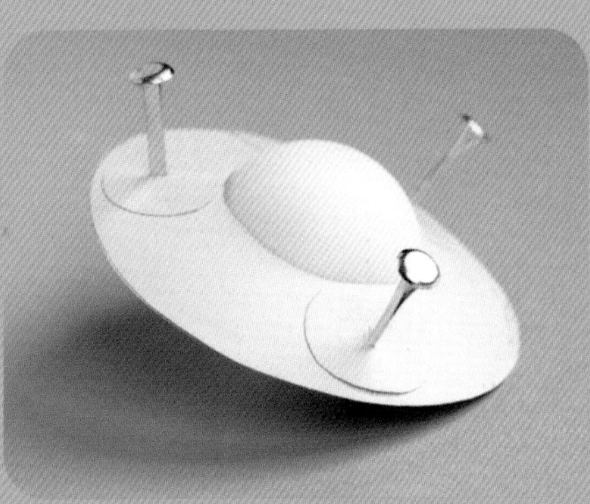

6 Attach the legs to the saucer by gluing the circle ends to the saucer ring. Make sure to space the legs evenly around.

7 Ask an adult to use pliers to straighten out a jumbo paper clip, and add a zigzag to the end. This shape will be easier to attach to the UFO than a straight shape. If the paper clip is difficult to bend, you could use thick craft wire instead.

8 Attach the zigzag to the underside of the saucer using sticky tape. Glue the last circle on top to hide it.

9 Pierce the bouncy ball with the other end of the paper clip to make a small hole, then push it in firmly.

10 Run your finger along the wire to find the place where the spaceship and bouncy ball are equally balanced. Mark this place (called the balance point) with a marker pen. Fold an M shape into the wire at the balance point.

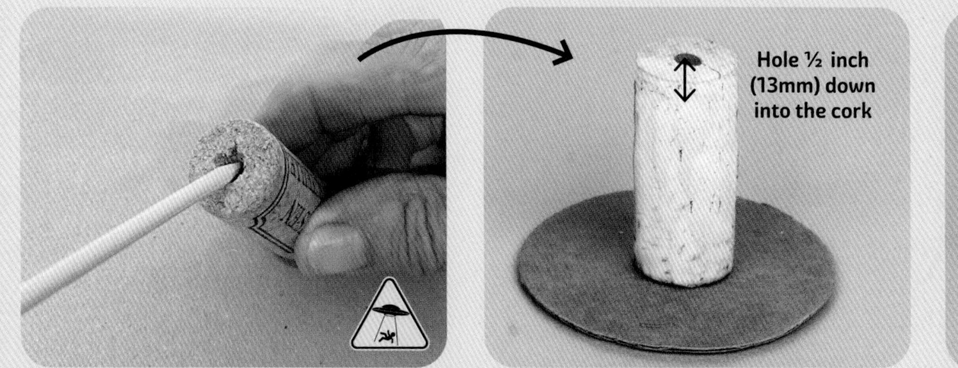

11 Dig out a small hole ½ inch (13mm) deep into the top of the cork, using a pointy skewer. The hole needs to be wide enough for a lollipop stick or paper straw to fit inside. Glue the cork to the middle of a circle of corrugated cardboard. The circle can be any size, this is just a base for the UFO.

12 Carefully cut a 1 inch (25mm) length from a lollipop stick or strong paper straw and fit it into the hole in the cork.

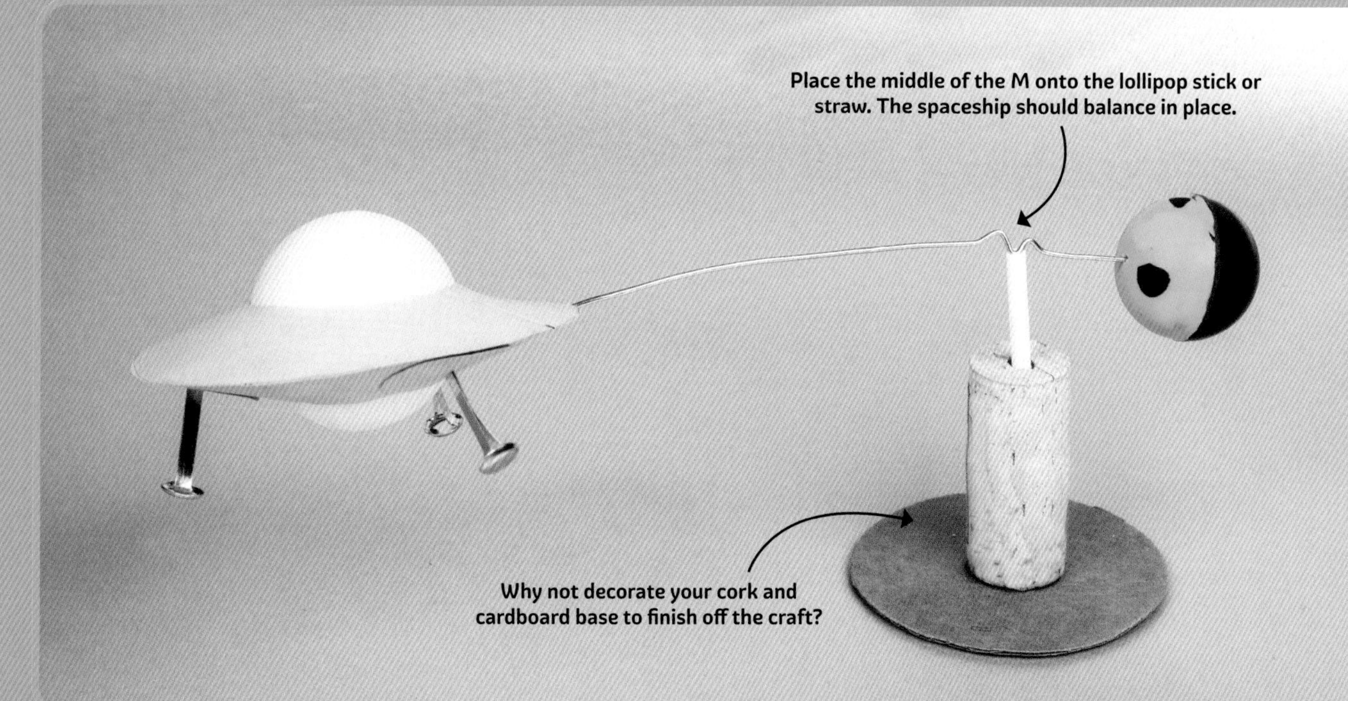

WATCH THE UFO HOVER MYSTERIOUSLY!

DID YOU KNOW?

UFO stands for Unidentified Flying Object. This can be anything in the sky that the person who saw it can't explain. Some people claim to have seen UFOs that look like alien spaceships, but no scientific evidence has been found to confirm alien life... yet!

DID YOU KNOW?

Scientists believe that for another planet to have **intelligent life** on it, it must be similar to Earth in a few ways. It probably needs an atmosphere (air), water, and light and heat caused by orbiting a star (like the Sun).

AMAZING SPACE EXPERIMENTS

The first astronomers came up with ideas about outer space. They didn't have the right equipment to put them to the test, but now modern scientists do!

LEARNING ABOUT PLANETS

For years, astronomers could only do experiments on Earth. They created models, like the Orbiting Orrery (page 54), to demonstrate the way that the planets move around the Sun. These scientific models help us understand what's happening in our solar system.

THE BIG QUESTIONS

Gravity was discovered in the 1600s when scientist Sir Isaac Newton questioned why an apple falls to the ground rather than floating upward or sideways! His work was revolutionary as it helped explain why the Moon keeps orbiting the Earth, and Earth keeps orbiting the Sun.

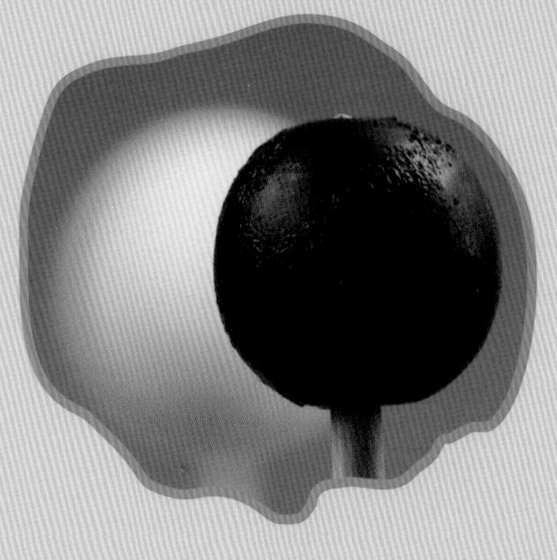

WANT TO KNOW MORE?

This chapter is full of amazing experiments. From watching how astronauts land back on Earth with an exciting eggs-periment to testing the power of a vacuum, there's lots of fun projects to try.

ORBITING ORRERY

Make this awesome moving model to see how Earth and its Moon orbit the Sun!

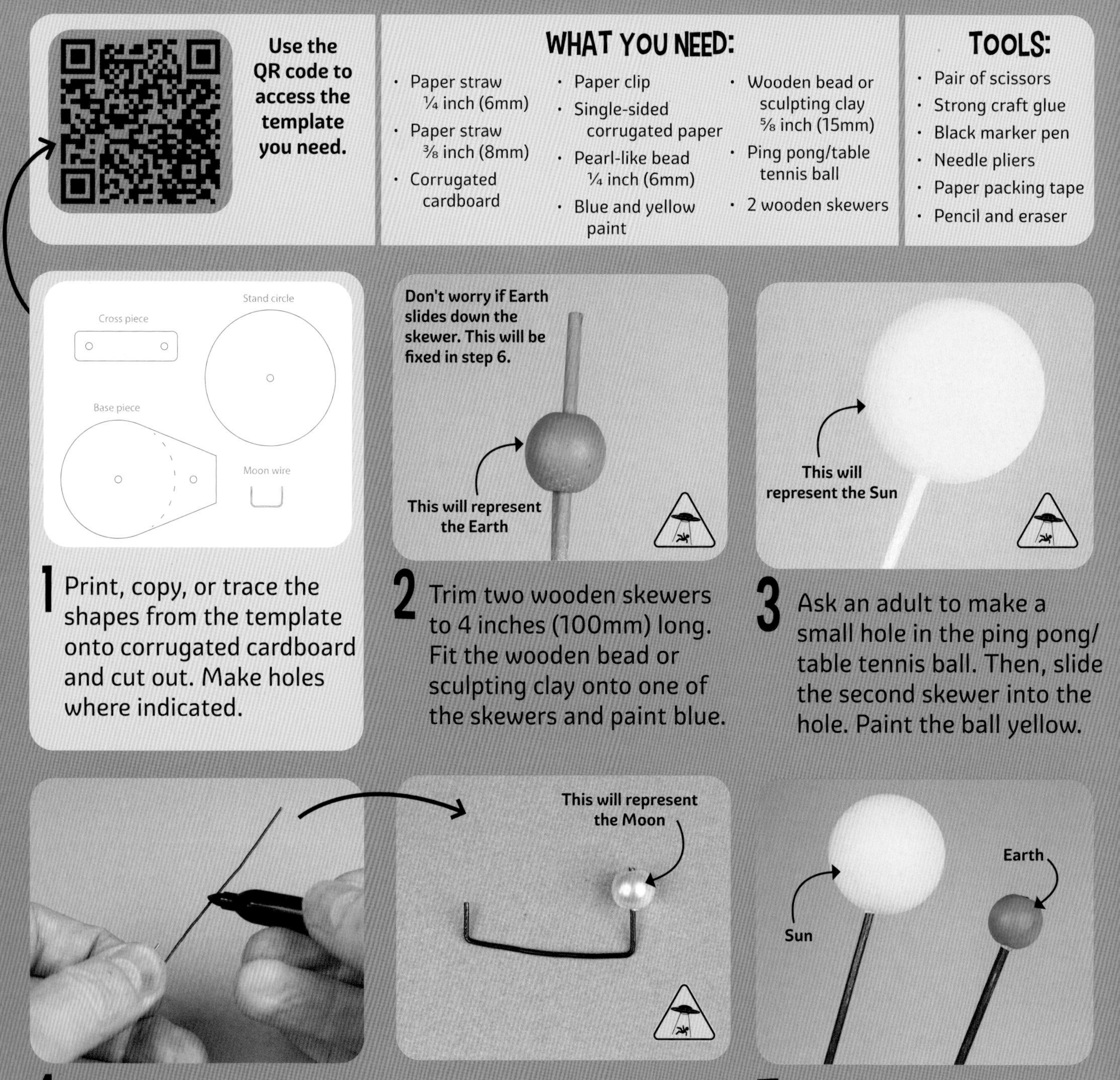

Use the QR code to access the template you need.

WHAT YOU NEED:

- Paper straw ¼ inch (6mm)
- Paper straw ⅜ inch (8mm)
- Corrugated cardboard
- Paper clip
- Single-sided corrugated paper
- Pearl-like bead ¼ inch (6mm)
- Blue and yellow paint
- Wooden bead or sculpting clay ⅝ inch (15mm)
- Ping pong/table tennis ball
- 2 wooden skewers

TOOLS:

- Pair of scissors
- Strong craft glue
- Black marker pen
- Needle pliers
- Paper packing tape
- Pencil and eraser

1 Print, copy, or trace the shapes from the template onto corrugated cardboard and cut out. Make holes where indicated.

2 Trim two wooden skewers to 4 inches (100mm) long. Fit the wooden bead or sculpting clay onto one of the skewers and paint blue.

3 Ask an adult to make a small hole in the ping pong/table tennis ball. Then, slide the second skewer into the hole. Paint the ball yellow.

4 Uncoil a paper clip, then shade it in with black marker pen. Ask an adult to bend the paper clip into the shape shown using pliers. Fit the pearl-like bead on top, gluing into place.

5 Shade in the Sun and Earth skewers with black marker pen.

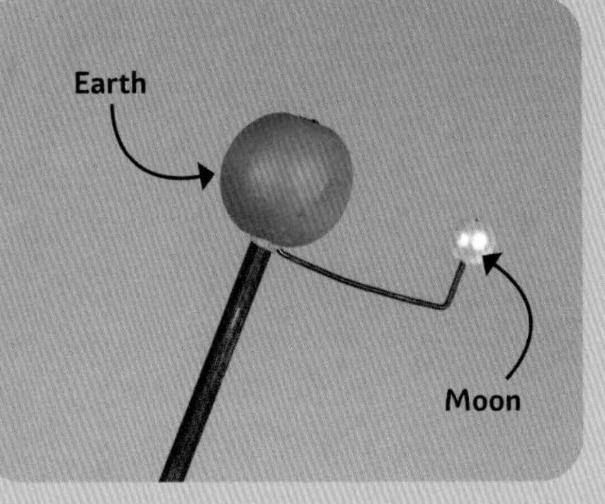

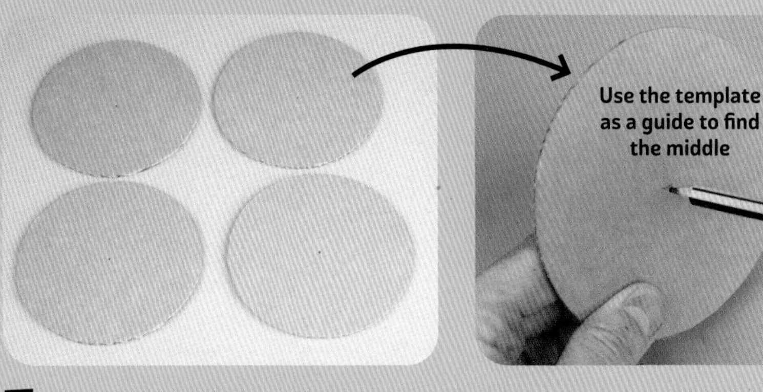

6 Make sure the Earth is at the top of the skewer, then slot the Moon's paper clip arm inside the bead. Glue both in place.

7 Make a small hole using a pencil and eraser (see page 11) in the middle of each corrugated cardboard circle from the template pieces. The hole should be just big enough for one of the narrower straws to fit inside.

8 Thread the circles onto straw A (¼ inch/6mm) so that they line up. Then, glue the circles together.

9 Cut a piece of single-sided corrugated paper to fit perfectly around the circular cardboard stand. Glue in place as shown.

10 Push straw A further into the stand so that it pokes out the same amount as the height of the base piece that you cut out from the template.

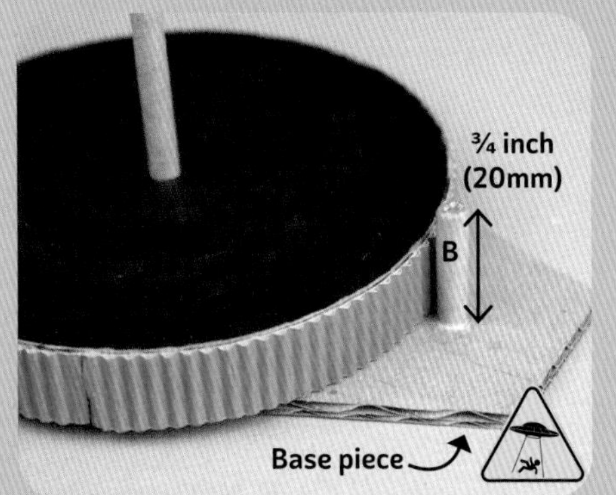

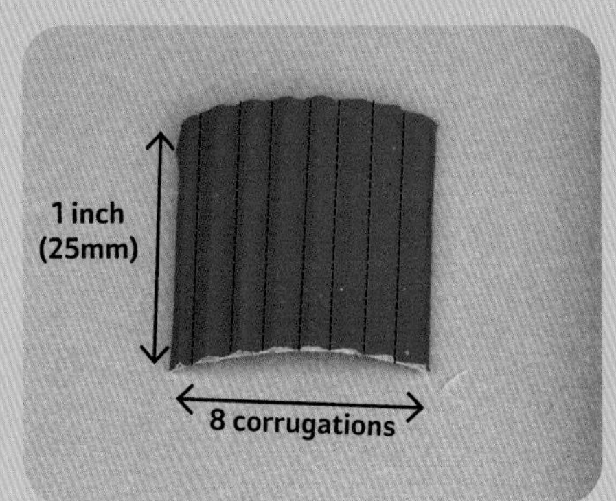

11 Slot the stand into the base where indicated on the template. It should still be able to turn freely. Decorate the stand with black marker.

12 Cut the other ¼ inch (6mm) straw (straw B) to ¾ inch (20mm) high. Then, glue it to the base where indicated on the template.

13 Cut a strip of single-sided corrugated paper to 1 inch (25mm) high and 8 corrugations wide.

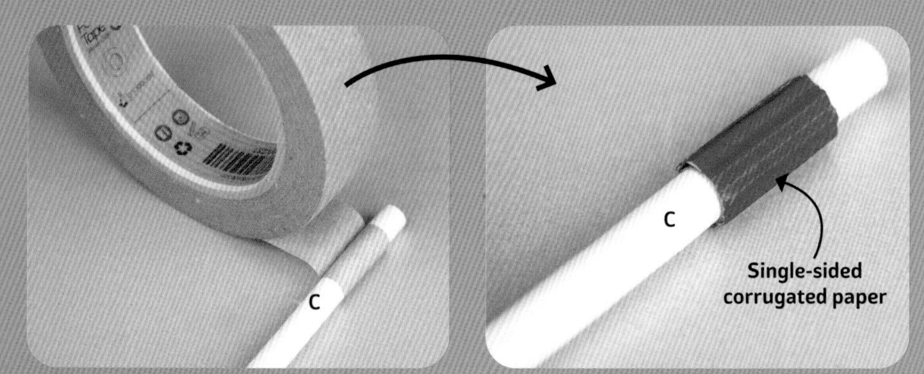

14 Roll tape around straw C ($\frac{3}{8}$ inch/8mm) until it's thick enough so that the single-sided corrugated paper wraps exactly around and the ends meet up. Glue together.

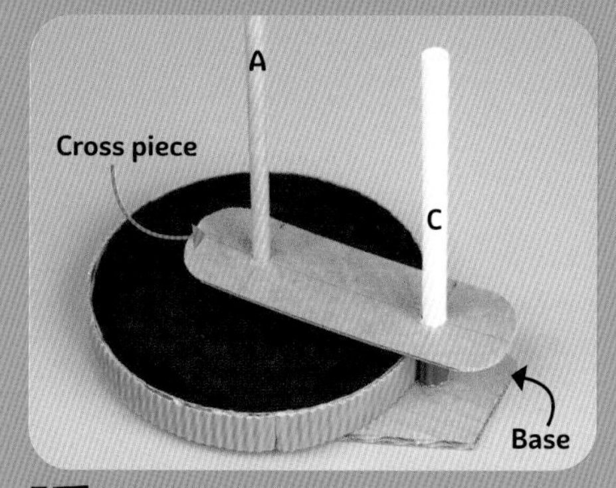

15 Slot straw C onto straw B, with the corrugated card at the bottom. Slide the cross piece from the template onto the straws as shown.

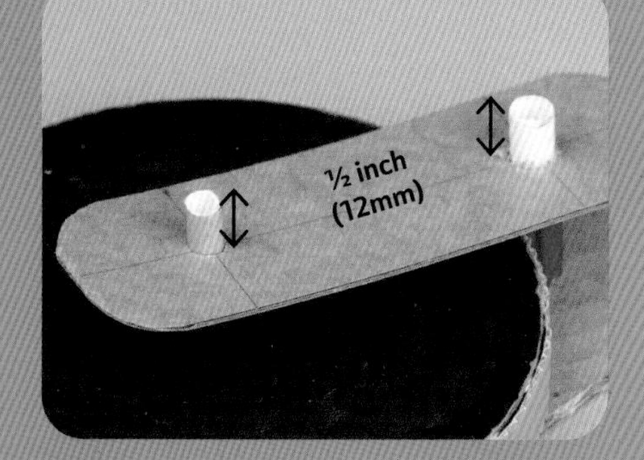

16 Trim straws A and C so that ½ inch (12mm) remains above the cross piece.

17 Tape around the Earth and Sun skewers so that when they're placed in the straws they stand upright.

18 Place the Earth and Moon skewer into straw C, and the Sun into straw A.

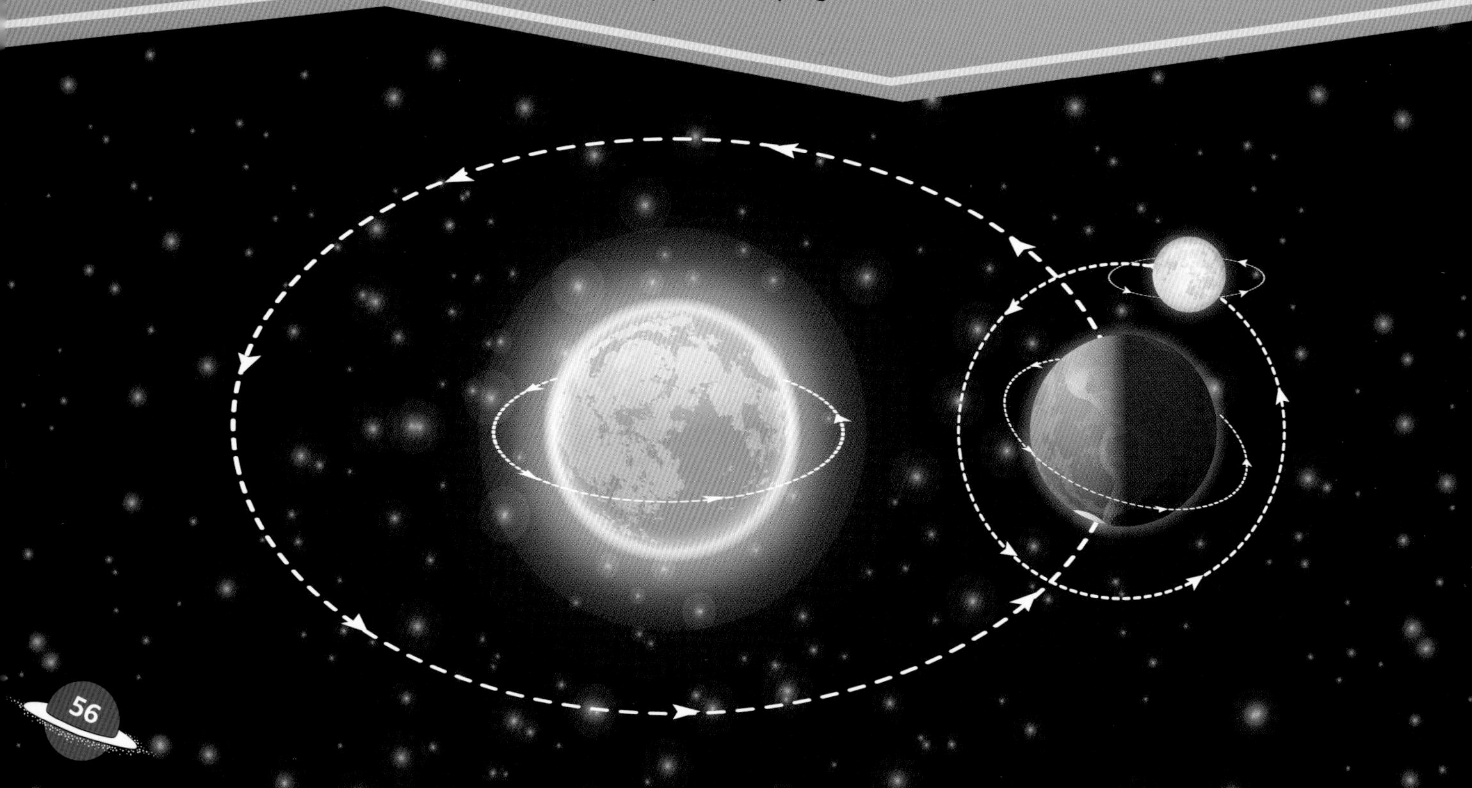

Guide piece

DID YOU KNOW?

In reality, it takes Earth 365 days - a whole year - to complete a full orbit of the Sun. During that time, the planet travels over 584 million miles (940 million km)! Our Moon follows, constantly spinning around Earth, too. What a journey!

SOLAR ECLIPSE

A solar eclipse happens when the Moon moves between Earth and the Sun, gradually blocking out the light from the Sun. You can understand how that is possible with this cool model!

WHAT YOU NEED:

- Ping pong/table tennis ball
- Yellow and black paint
- Wooden bead or sculpting clay ½ inch (12mm) across
- Bamboo skewers
- Corrugated cardboard
- Felt-tip pens or pencils (optional)

TOOLS:

- Ruler
- Pair of scissors
- Strong craft glue

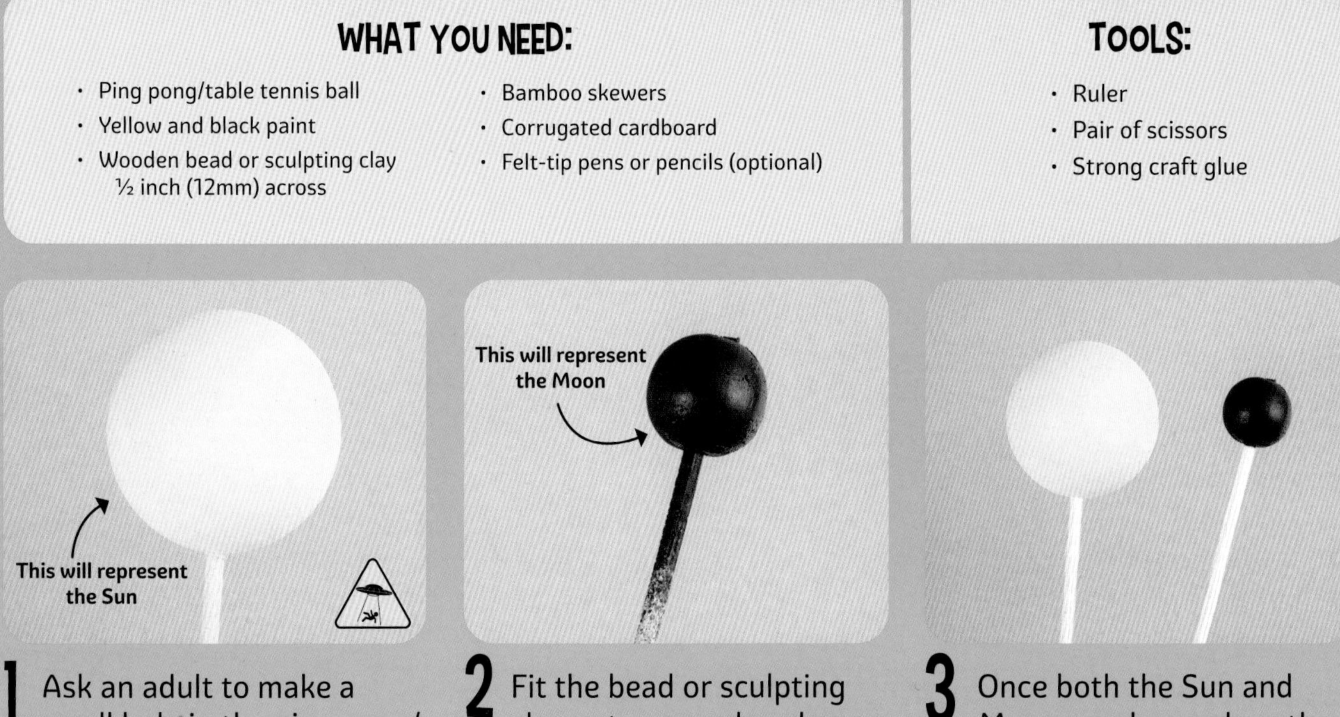

1 Ask an adult to make a small hole in the ping pong/ table tennis ball. Slide a wooden skewer into the hole. Paint the ball yellow.

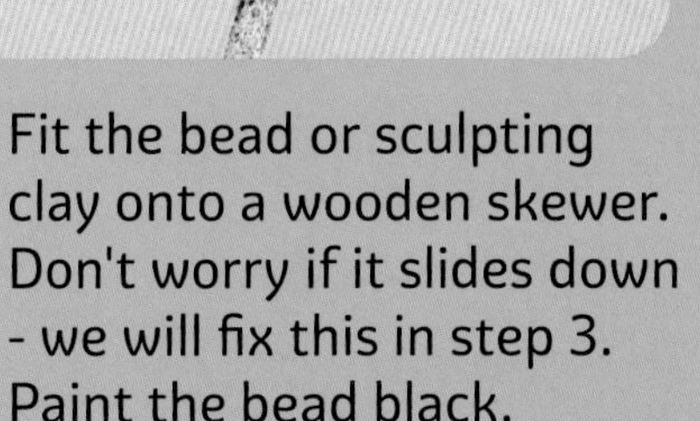

2 Fit the bead or sculpting clay onto a wooden skewer. Don't worry if it slides down - we will fix this in step 3. Paint the bead black.

3 Once both the Sun and Moon are dry, replace the skewers with clean ones. Glue in place to secure.

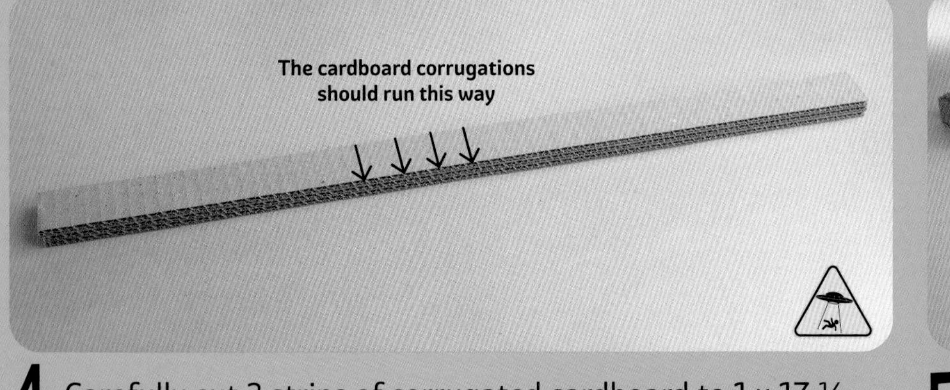

Why not decorate the cardboard strip using felt-tip pens?

4 Carefully cut 3 strips of corrugated cardboard to 1 x 17 ½ inches (25mm x 450mm) with the corrugations running in the direction shown. Glue the cardboard strips together, making one thick strip.

5 Turn the cardboard strip to stand on its long, thin edge. Fit the Sun at one end and the Moon at the other.

How to use your solar eclipse model:

1. Position your eye (or camera) in line with the model.

2. With the Moon closest to you, move your head (or camera) right to left to see the phases of an eclipse.

This is a partial eclipse

This is when the Moon covers part of the Sun.

This is a total eclipse

This is when the Moon completely covers the Sun.

DID YOU KNOW?

The Moon doesn't make its own light but reflects the light of the Sun. Why not paint your Moon half yellow and half black (vertically) to show which side of the Moon is facing the Sun?

EGG-CELLENT PARACHUTE

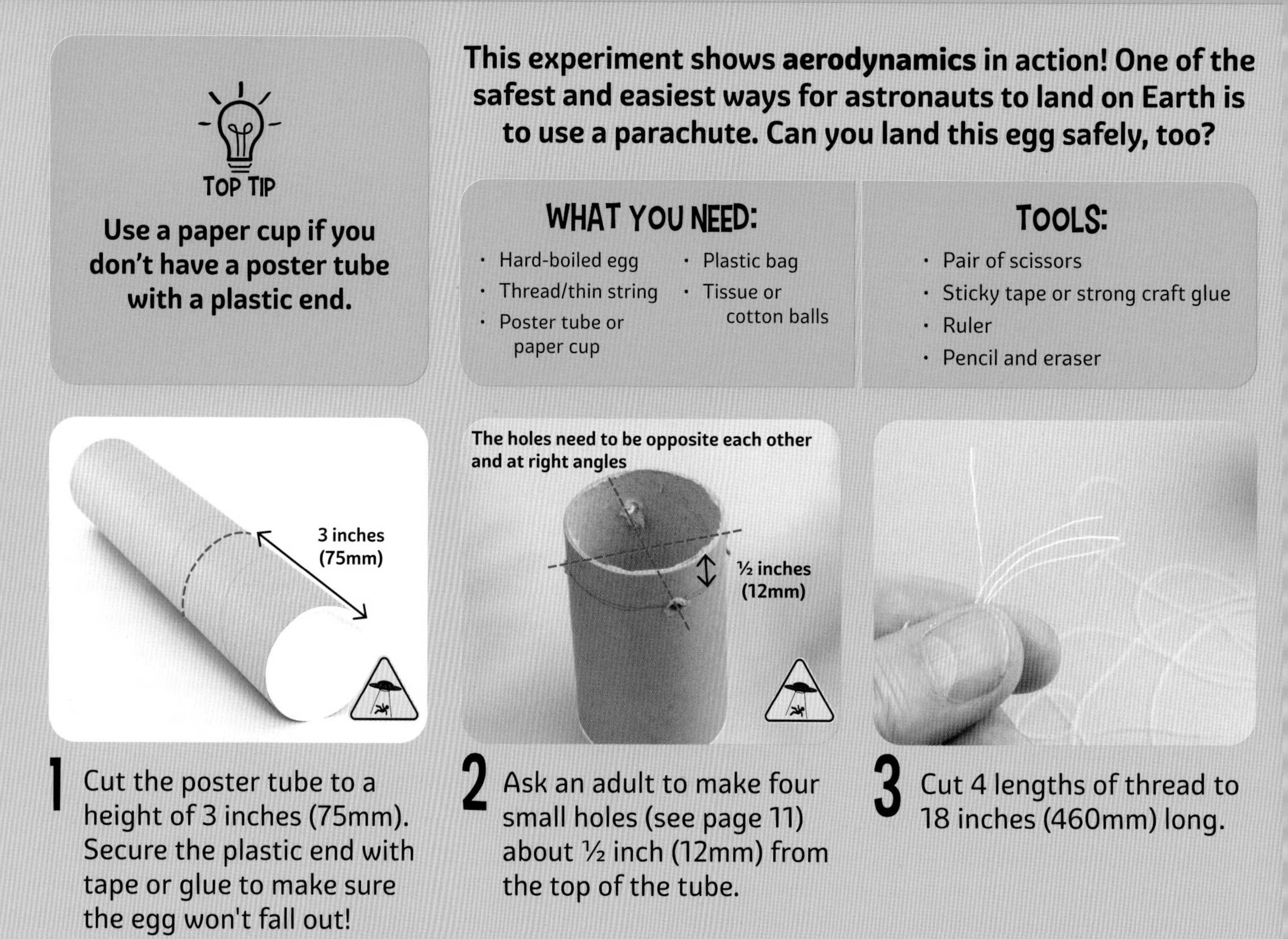

This experiment shows aerodynamics in action! One of the safest and easiest ways for astronauts to land on Earth is to use a parachute. Can you land this egg safely, too?

TOP TIP

Use a paper cup if you don't have a poster tube with a plastic end.

WHAT YOU NEED:

- Hard-boiled egg
- Thread/thin string
- Poster tube or paper cup
- Plastic bag
- Tissue or cotton balls

TOOLS:

- Pair of scissors
- Sticky tape or strong craft glue
- Ruler
- Pencil and eraser

1 Cut the poster tube to a height of 3 inches (75mm). Secure the plastic end with tape or glue to make sure the egg won't fall out!

2 Ask an adult to make four small holes (see page 11) about ½ inch (12mm) from the top of the tube.

3 Cut 4 lengths of thread to 18 inches (460mm) long.

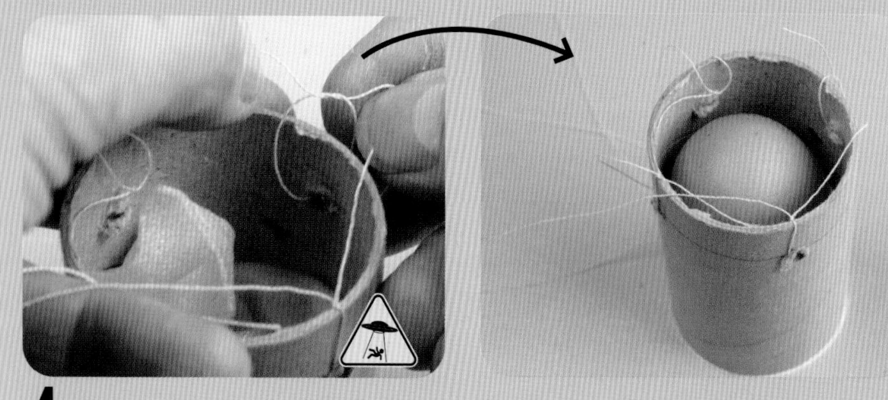

4 Take one piece of thread and tie it to a hole in the poster tube. Repeat until each hole has a piece of thread tied to it. Place some tissue or cotton balls inside followed by the egg.

TOP TIP

Make sure you tie strong double knots in this craft to hold everything together. Ask an adult to help you to make sure they are secure!

5 Cut a piece of plastic bag roughly 18 inches (460mm) square to make the parachute.

6 Pair up each piece of thread with one corner of the plastic bag. Tie the thread tightly to its corner.

HOW DOES THIS WORK?

As the egg is pulled toward the surface of the Earth by gravity, a strong force produced by air resistance pushes upward against the parachute. This reduces the force of gravity and slows the egg's fall.

7 Fill the top of the poster tube with tissue or cotton balls to keep the egg in place.

THROW THE PARACHUTE AS HIGH AS YOU CAN AND WATCH IT DRIFT SAFELY BACK DOWN TO EARTH!

ROCKET POWER

Watch this car shoot off as the balloon loses air. This exciting experiment uses the same principle as rocket power: a thrust backward creates a surge forward.

WHAT YOU NEED:

- A balloon
- Marker pen ½ inch (12mm) wide
- 4 wooden beads ½ inch (12mm)
- 2 wooden skewers
- Poster tube 2 inches (50mm) in diameter
- 4 circular plastic lids 3 inches (75mm) in diameter
- 2 cable ties

TOOLS:

- Ruler
- Pencil
- Eraser
- Pair of scissors
- Sticky tape
- Craft knife

1 Ask an adult to cut a poster tube to 8 inches (200mm) long (see page 10) and make holes slightly larger than the skewers on opposite sides, about 1 ½ inches (40mm) from each end. If these holes are too small, your car won't move very well. Don't worry; you can test this out in step 4.

2 Cut the skewers to 3 ½ inches (90mm), then thread them through the holes in the tube. Add a bead on each side as a washer.

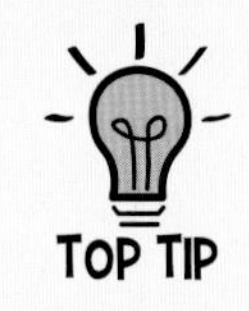

TOP TIP

The plastic lid from potato chip/crisp containers are the perfect size for the wheels! Better start eating; you need four lids!

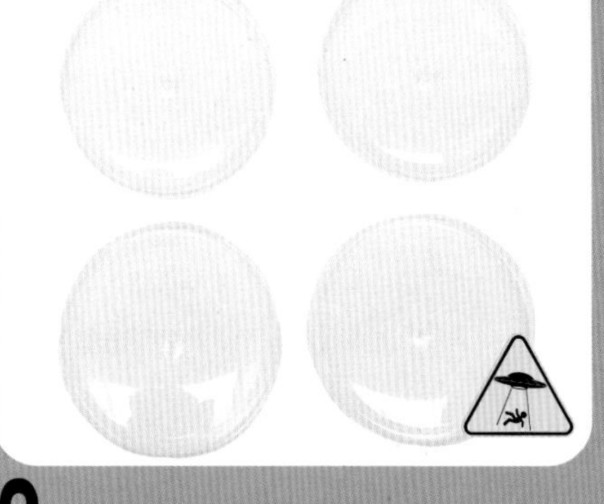

3 Ask an adult to make a small hole in the middle of each lid to fit the skewer through tightly.

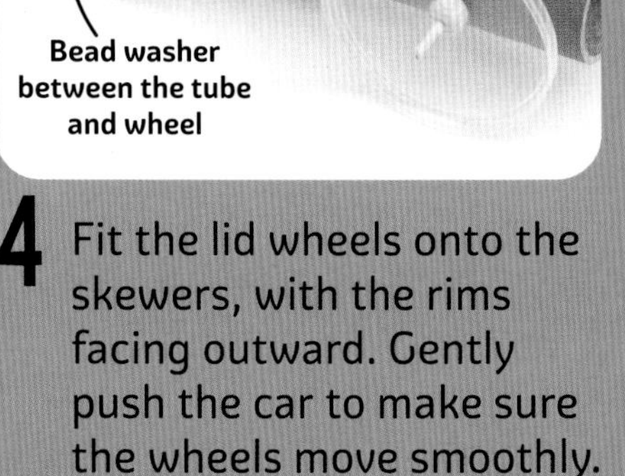

4 Fit the lid wheels onto the skewers, with the rims facing outward. Gently push the car to make sure the wheels move smoothly.

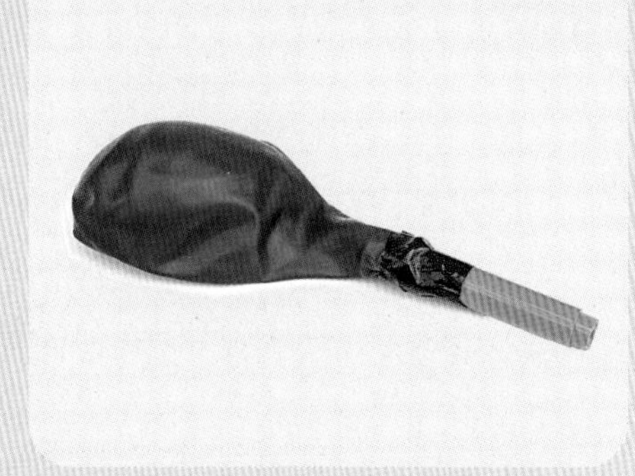

5 Ask an adult to cut the pen body to 2 ¾ inches (70mm). The inside should drop out. Fit the end of the balloon over one end of the pen and tape in place. Blow into the pen to inflate the balloon and check no air escapes from the tape.

6 Position the pen on the poster tube so that it extends beyond the end by ½ inch (12mm).

BLOW THE BALLOON UP, PINCH IT ABOVE THE STRAW, PLACE IT DOWN, AND RELEASE!

WEIGHT SLIDE RULER

Did you know that light things, like this book, would weigh more on other planets? Use this fun slide ruler to work out weight across the solar system!

Use the QR code to access the template you need.

WHAT YOU NEED:

- Corrugated cardboard
- Thin cardstock/card
- Plain white paper
- Clear plastic sheet
- Black marker pen

TOOLS:

- Ruler
- Pair of scissors
- Strong craft glue
- Sticky tape

1 Print, copy, or trace the shapes from the template onto the specified materials and cut out.

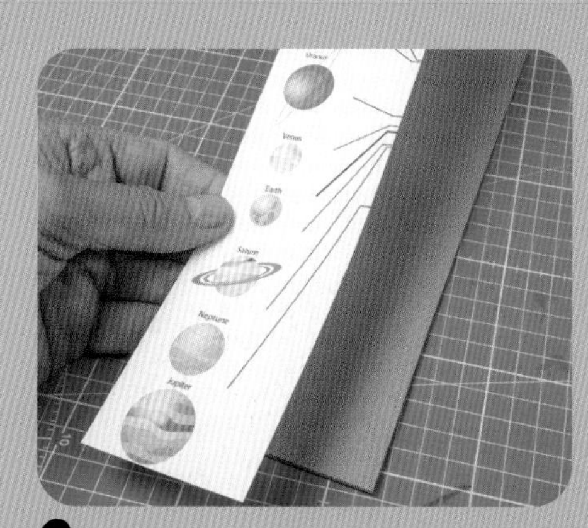

2 Glue the three paper parts from the template on top of their corresponding corrugated cardboard part.

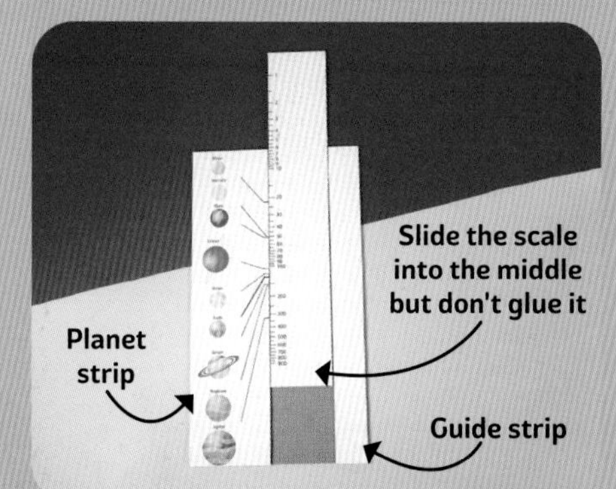

3 Glue the planet strips onto the backboard with the left sides lined up. Then, glue the guide strip onto the backboard with the right sides lined up.

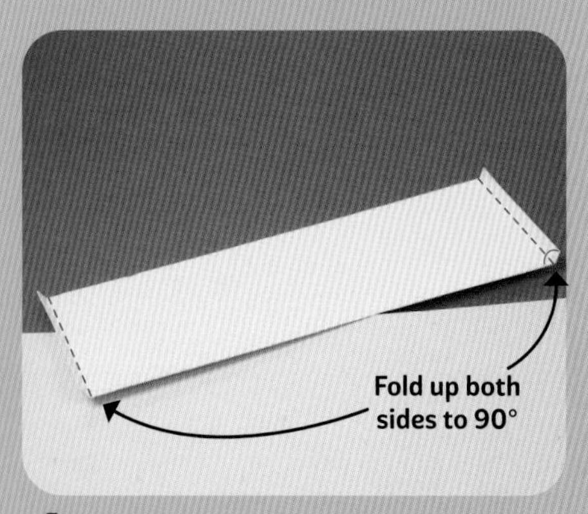

4 To make the cursor, take the cardstock/card cursor piece from the template. Score (see page 11) then fold along the dotted lines.

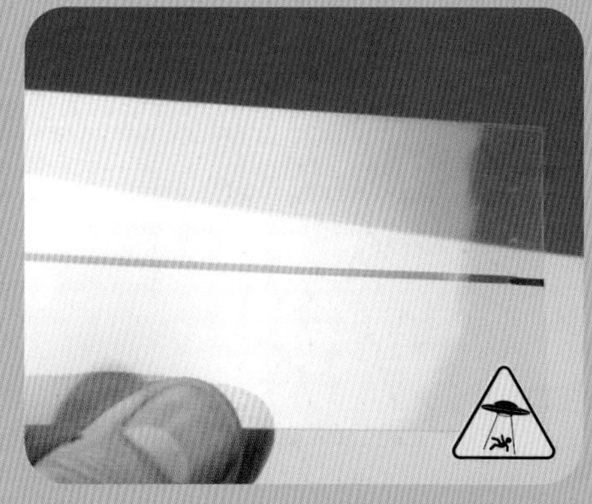

5 Cut out a piece of clear plastic using the cursor front template. Measure and mark a horizontal line through the middle with a black marker pen.

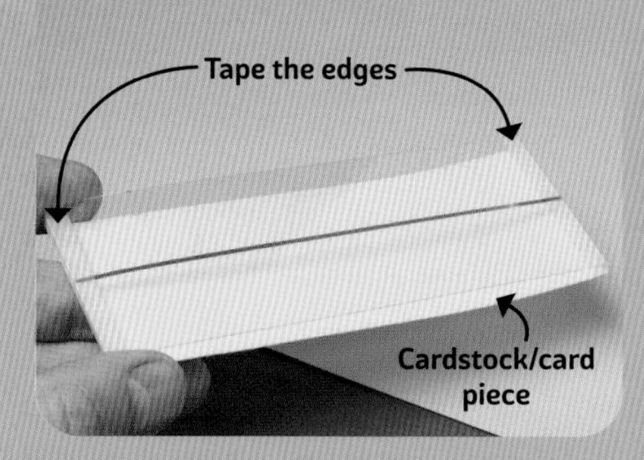

6 Balance the plastic on the folded sides of the cardstock/card piece and tape the edges where they meet to complete the cursor.

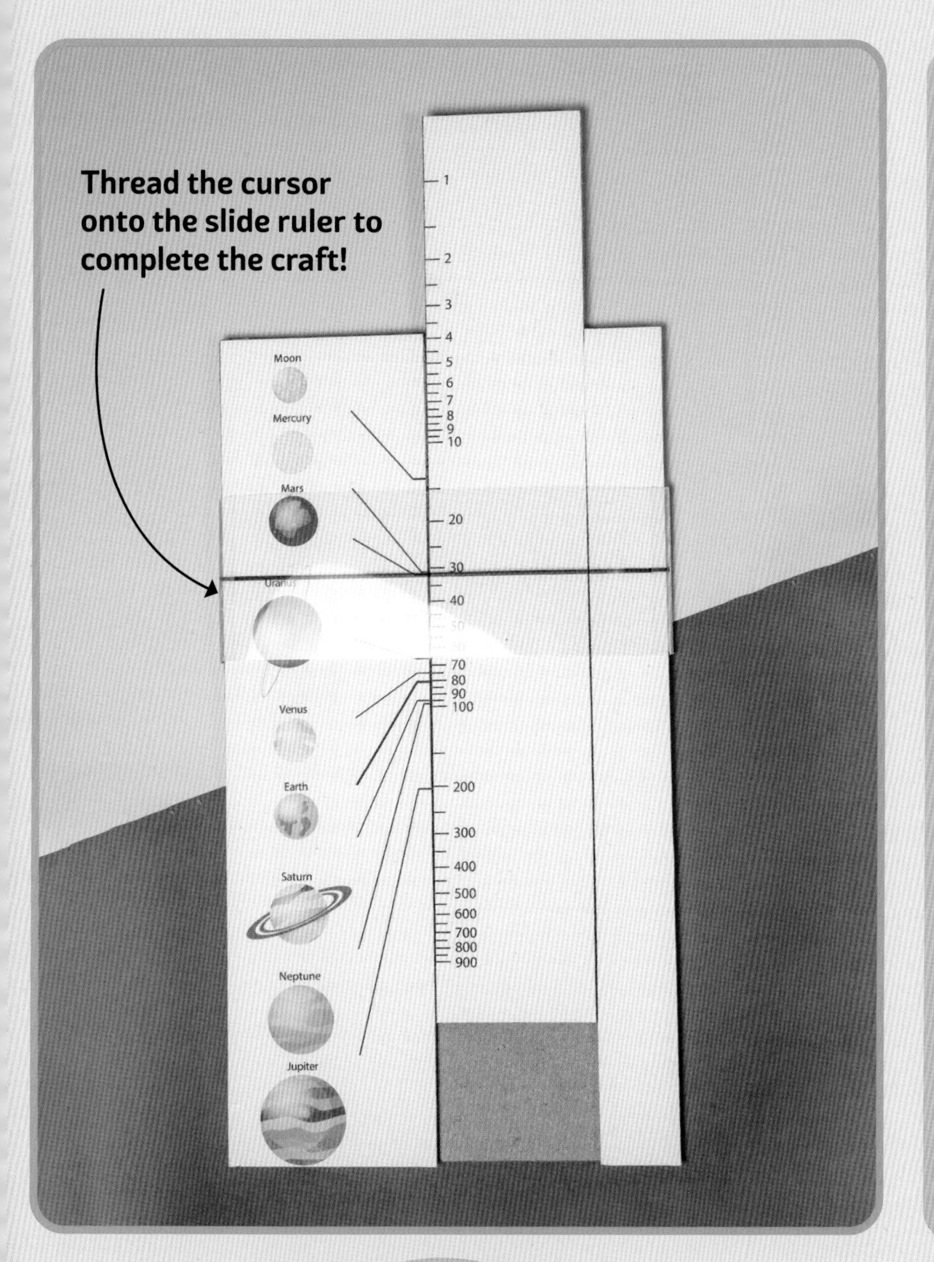

How to use your weight slide ruler:

1.
Line up the scale so that Earth is pointing to the weight of the item.

2.
Without moving the scale, read what the weight would be on the other planets.

Example:

If something weighs 80lbs (36kg) on Earth, it would only weigh about 14lbs (6kg) on the Moon, but on Jupiter it would weigh over 200lbs (90kg)!

Have fun working out what different things would weigh on the different planets. Why not try the following:

- This book
- Shoe
- Phone
- Toy

DID YOU KNOW?

Weight is a combination of an item's mass (everything something's made of) and the strength of gravity on the planet (the force keeping your feet on the ground). An item's shape and size stay the same from planet to planet, but because each planet has a different gravity strength, it would appear lighter or heavier depending on where it is!

VACUUM EXPERIMENT

Outer space is a vacuum – there's no air! Create the vacuum of outer space down here on Earth with this extraordinary experiment.

WHAT YOU NEED:

- Large syringe with plastic tube
- Small glass jar
- Marshmallows

TOOLS:

- Pair of scissors
- Glue gun (cool melt) or strong craft glue

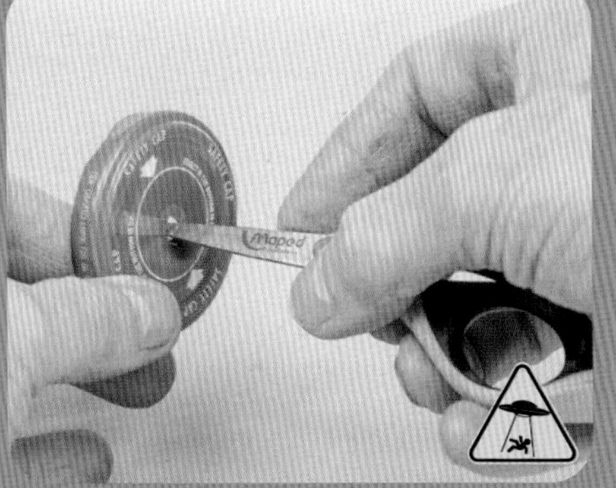

1 Ask an adult to make a hole in the lid of the jar - **don't do this yourself!** It needs to be big enough for the plastic tube to fit through.

2 Thread the end of the plastic tube through the hole and seal with glue.

3 Fill the jar with marshmallows, then screw the lid on tightly. Attach the syringe to the tube.

DID YOU KNOW?

By removing all the air from the jar, we create a vacuum. You can see what happens to the marshmallows with even a little of the air removed. Imagine what would happen to them in the vacuum of outer space!

PULL THE SYRINGE TO SEE THE MARSHMALLOWS EXPAND!

SUPER SOLAR SYSTEM MODEL

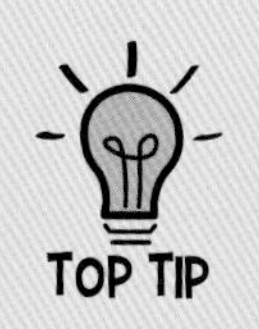

TOP TIP

Make up a funny rhyme to help you remember the order of the planets in our solar system.

Have fun making the solar system out of clay and see just how small Earth is compared to Jupiter!

WHAT YOU NEED:

- Ball 9 inches (230mm) across
- Assorted sculpting clay
- Small paper clips
- Assorted cardstock/card

TOOLS:

- Plastic knife or sturdy ruler (for cutting clay)
- Strong craft glue
- Ruler
- Pair of scissors
- Needle pliers

JUPITER is identifiable by its banded cloud.

1 Roll out brown, yellow, and orange sculpting clay and stack on top of each other.

2 Slice off the edges of the pile to create a rough cylinder.

3 Shape the clay into a ball 1 inch (24mm) across.

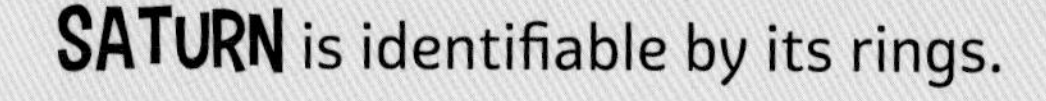

SATURN is identifiable by its rings.

1 Make a brownish ball of sculpting clay ¾ inch (20mm) across.

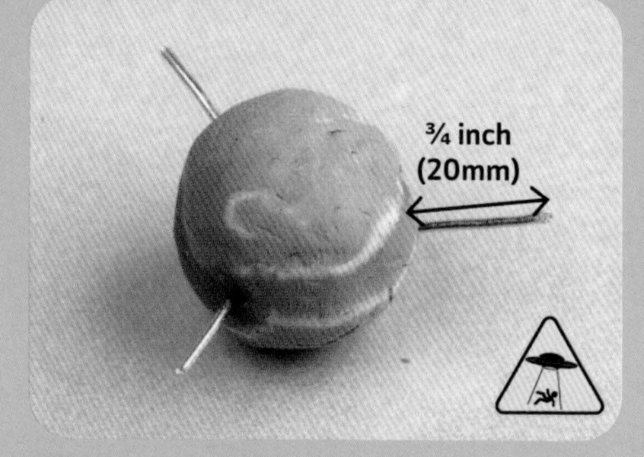

2 Straighten out three small paper clips and insert into the clay ball an equal distance apart.

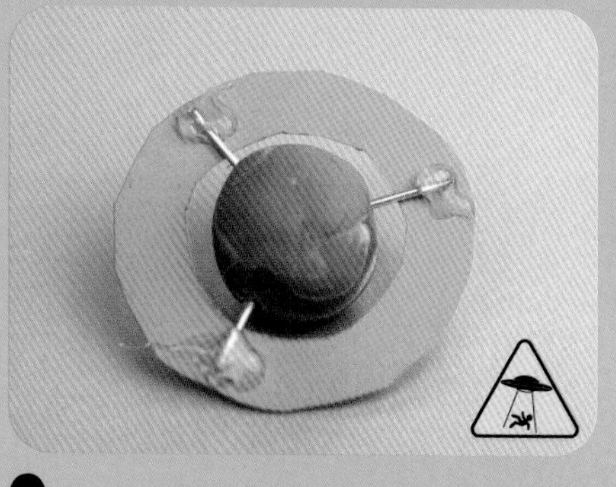

3 Cut out a ring of cardstock/card. Glue the ring to the paper clips as shown. Then, flip over to hide the ends.

HAVE FUN MAKING THE OTHER PLANETS!

Use this helpful chart to make sure your planets are to scale with each other:

PLANET	CLAY	SIZE
Mercury	Brown and yellow	1⁄16 inch (1mm)
Venus	Yellow and orange	1⁄8 inch (2mm)
Earth	Blue, green, and white	1⁄8 inch (2mm)
Mars	Red	1⁄16 inch (1mm)
Jupiter	Brown, yellow, and orange	1 inch (24mm)
Saturn	Brown and orange	3⁄4 inch (20mm)
Uranus	Blue (light)	1⁄4 inch (7mm)
Neptune	Blue (dark)	1⁄4 inch (7mm)

Can you name these planets in order, based on what you've learned?

Use a basketball (9 inches/230mm) as the Sun when scaling up your planets.

TOP TIP

Why not make a stand for your solar system to display it on? Fold a piece of cardboard on a right angle, paint it black, and decorate with stars. Then, place your planets on top. **Scan the QR code to download and print the planet names to glue on, too!**

DID YOU KNOW?

All the planets in our solar system take a different amount of time to orbit the Sun. The closest to the Sun, Mercury, takes 88 Earth days. The furthest, Neptune, takes 60,190 Earth days - that's 165 Earth years!

SPECTACULAR SPACE PROJECTS

Outer space is an amazing place that we're learning more about thanks to scientists making bigger and better machines to explore space with. But we still have lots of questions!

AMAZING ASTRONAUTS

100 years ago, we didn't have the technology to travel into space, but now astronauts exist, and live and work 250 miles (over 400km) above the Earth on the **International Space Station (ISS).** These brave people make incredible discoveries from space!

SPACE ROBOTS

Scientists are always creating new robots to send to space. They are incredibly helpful for space exploration because they can go to planets that humans can't. We are learning a lot thanks to these fantastic exploring robots!

WANT TO KNOW MORE?

This chapter is full of super space-themed crafts to get your imagination running, as you wonder what it would be like to explore faraway planets and galaxies.

PENDULUM ASTRONAUT

Make this amazing astronaut on a pendulum and watch it swing from side to side, as if free-falling through space!

Use the QR code to access the template you need.

WHAT YOU NEED:

- Paper cup
- Bamboo skewer
- Small coins
- Coffee stirrer
- Paper straw
- Stiff black and white cardstock/card
- Craft stick
- Felt-tip pens or pencils

TOOLS:

- Pencil and eraser
- Ruler
- Pair of scissors
- Strong craft glue
- White paint marker pen

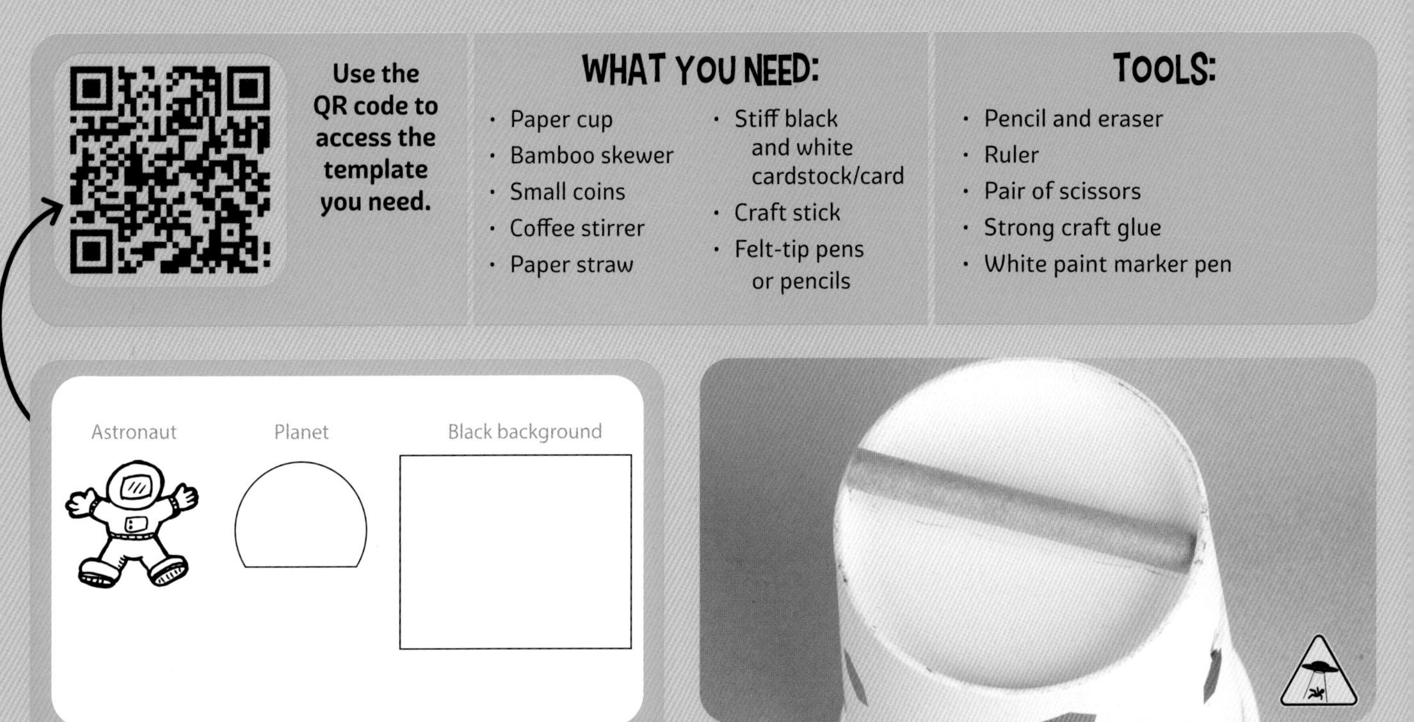

1 Print, copy, or trace the shapes from the template onto the specified materials and cut out. Decorate the planet and astronaut with felt-tip pens or pencils.

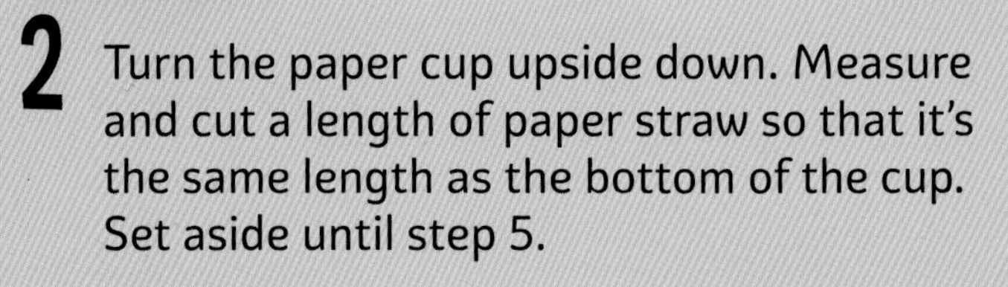

2 Turn the paper cup upside down. Measure and cut a length of paper straw so that it's the same length as the bottom of the cup. Set aside until step 5.

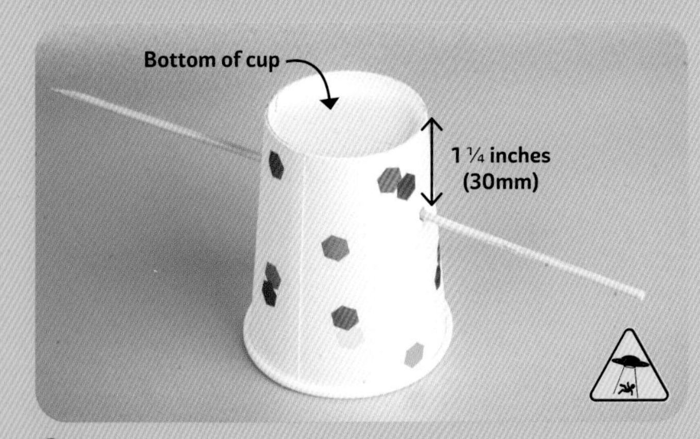

3 Make holes (see page 11) on either side of the cup, 1 ¼ inches (30mm) from the bottom. Push skewer through to check the holes line up, then trim so that ½ inch (12mm) remains at each side. Remove the skewer until step 8.

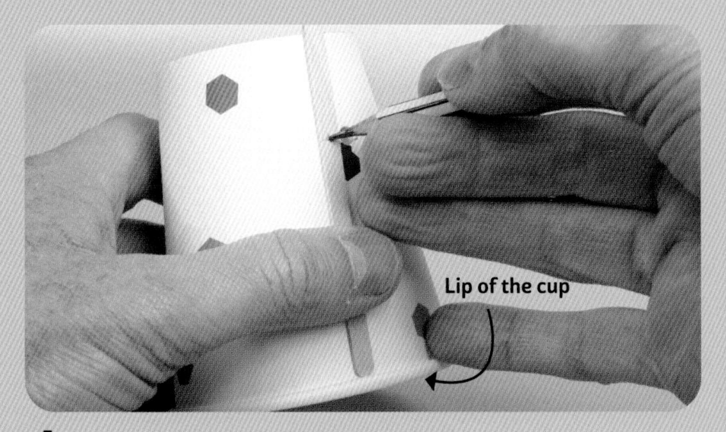

4 Hold the coffee stirrer so that the end touches the lip of the cup. Use a pencil to mark the stirrer where it lines up with the hole in the cup.

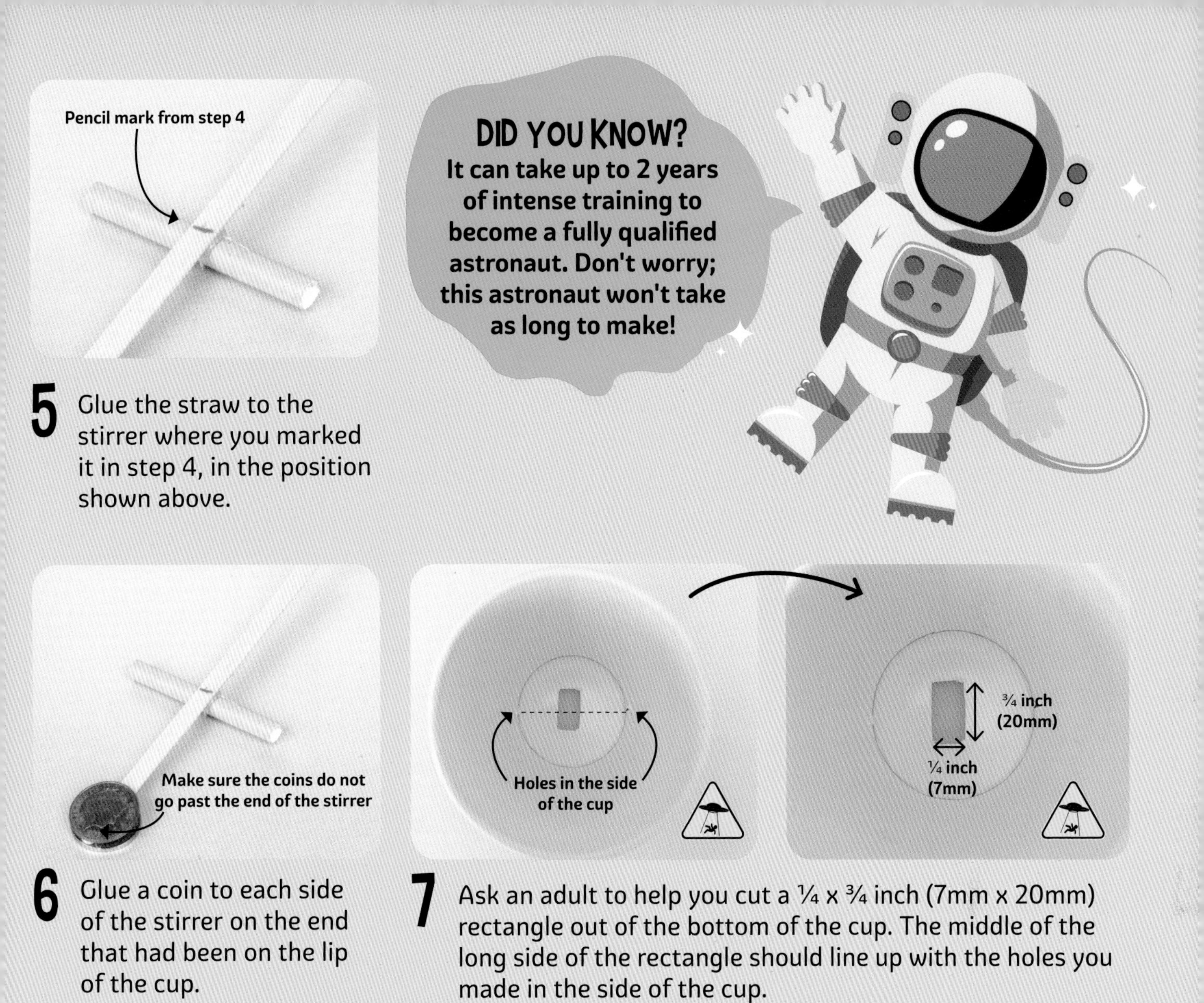

5 Glue the straw to the stirrer where you marked it in step 4, in the position shown above.

6 Glue a coin to each side of the stirrer on the end that had been on the lip of the cup.

7 Ask an adult to help you cut a ¼ x ¾ inch (7mm x 20mm) rectangle out of the bottom of the cup. The middle of the long side of the rectangle should line up with the holes you made in the side of the cup.

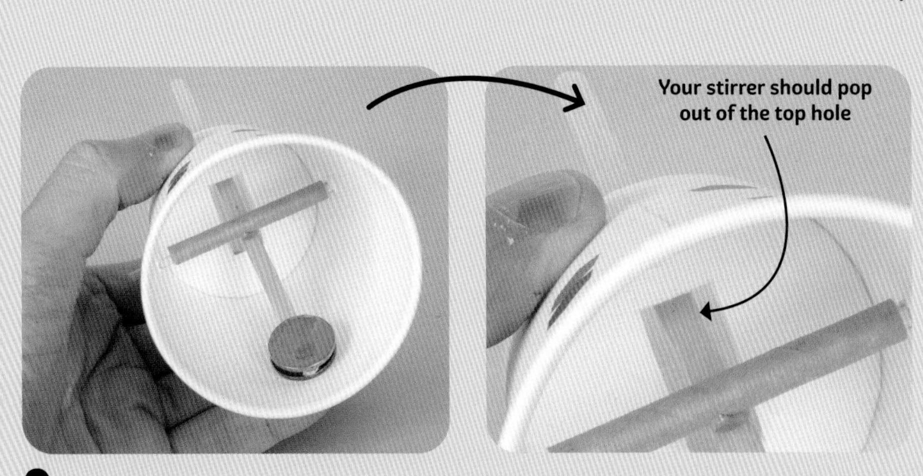

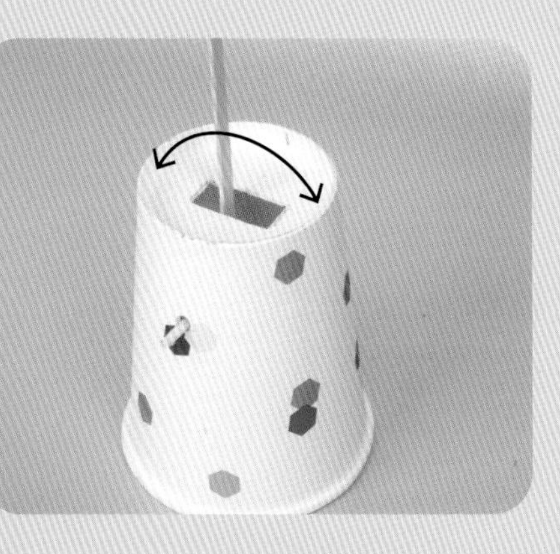

8 Thread the stirrer and straw up into the cup, with the coins pointing toward the lip of the cup. Line the straw up with the holes and thread the skewer through to hold it in place.

9 Glue the skewers into place. The stirrer should still be free to swing back and forth like a pendulum.

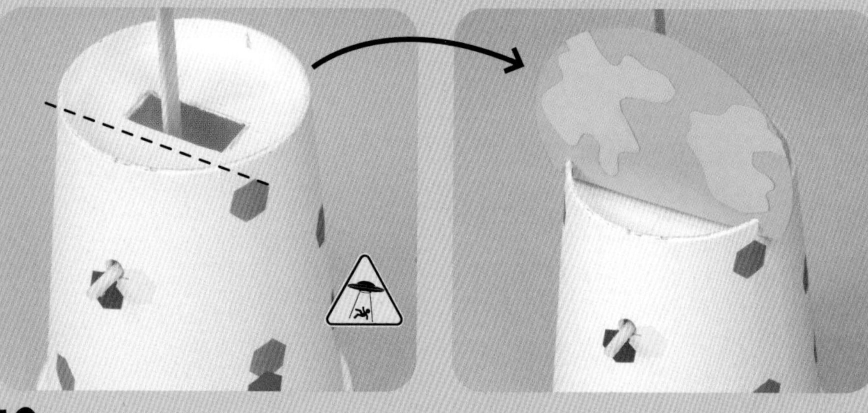

10 Make two small cuts near the front of the cup. They should be parallel with the long side of the rectangular hole and halfway between this and the front of the cup as shown. Then, fit your planet in. It shouldn't touch the stirrer.

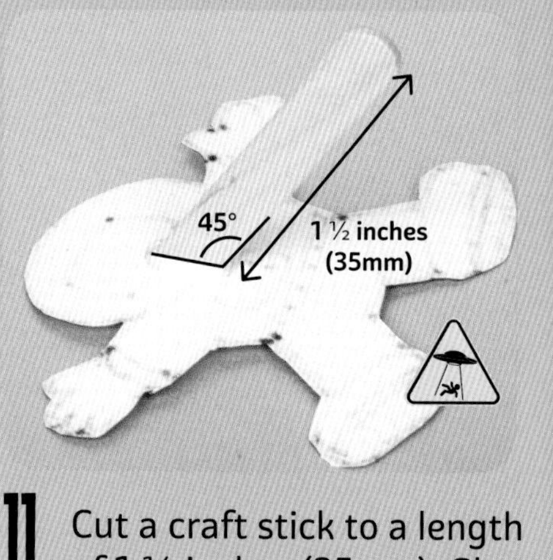

11 Cut a craft stick to a length of 1 ½ inches (35mm). Glue the angled end to the back of the astronaut from the template as shown.

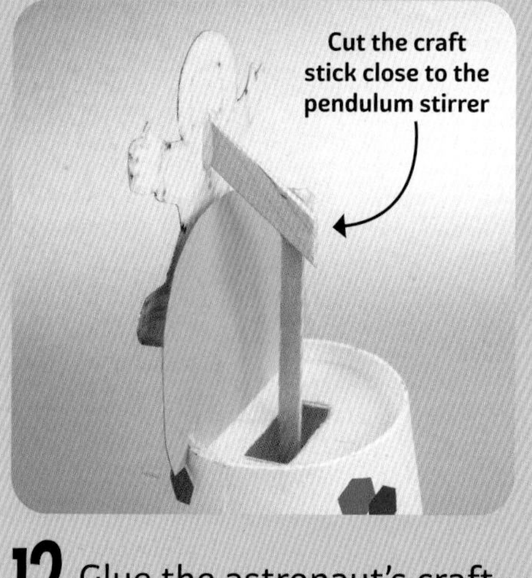

12 Glue the astronaut's craft stick to the pendulum stirrer so it can swing without touching the planet as shown.

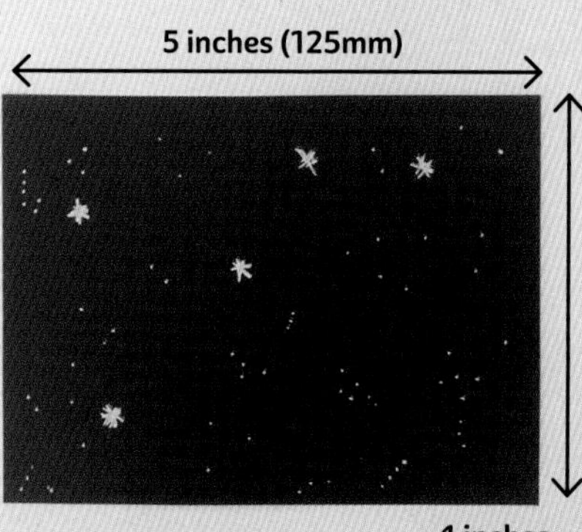

13 Cut a piece of stiff black cardstock/card to 5 x 4 inches (125 x 100mm). Create a **star field** with a white paint marker.

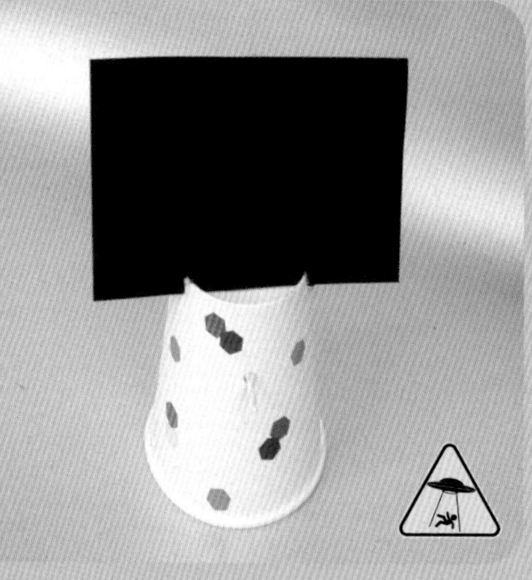

14 Make two small cuts near the back of the cup, behind the pendulum. Fit the black card in, making sure everything remains free to move.

DID YOU KNOW?

Astronauts sometimes complete spacewalks. This means they get out of their spacecraft while in space! They do this to carry out experiments, or repair satellites or spacecraft.

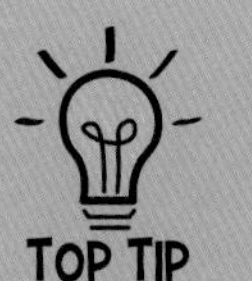

TOP TIP

Decorate your cup and astronaut however you like!

TAP THE ASTRONAUT TO SET THE PENDULUM SWINGING FROM SIDE TO SIDE!

PIPE CLEANER ALIENS

Making glittery aliens is a fun project to stretch your imagination. Here are a few examples you can try to get you going!

WHAT YOU NEED:

- Assorted tinsel pipe cleaners
- Corrugated cardboard
- Pom poms (assorted sizes)
- Plastic eyes

TOOLS:

- Pencil/pen (for curling the pipe cleaners)
- Pair of scissors
- Strong craft glue

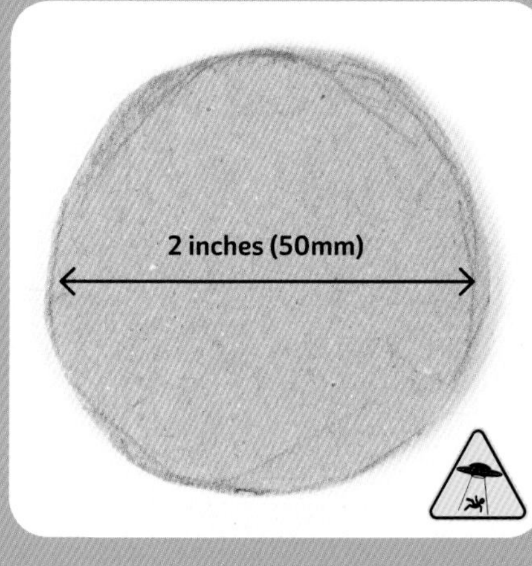

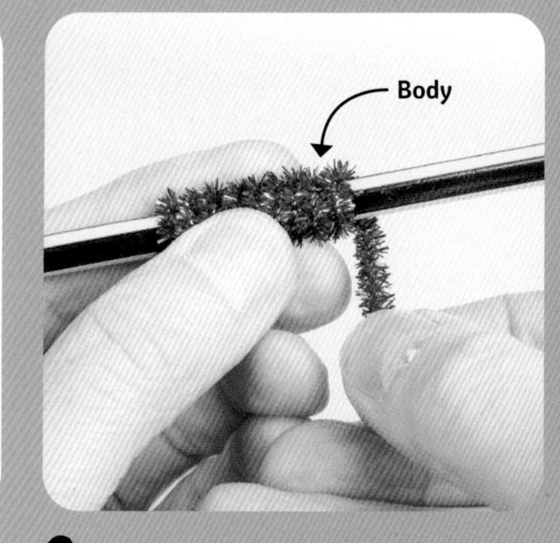

1 Cut out a small circle of corrugated cardboard, 2 inches (50mm) in diameter.

2 Wrap a tinsel pipe cleaner around a pencil, then slide it off. This will be the body.

3 Use strong glue to stick the alien's body to the middle of the cardboard circle.

4 Wrap a pipe cleaner once around the body, horizontally, leaving the two ends sticking out like arms as shown.

5 Glue on small pom poms to make the alien's hands. Glue on a larger pom pom to make the alien's head.

6 Make an eye stalk with another pipe cleaner, cutting it to a shorter size if you like. Glue a plastic eye to the end. Repeat to make a second.

7 Glue the eye stalks to the alien's head to complete the first alien.

TOP TIP

Try making other designs with different numbers of eyes, heads, and arms! How strange can you make them look?

LET YOUR IMAGINATION RUN WILD AS YOU MAKE YOUR OWN DESIGNS!

PULL-THE-TAB ROCKET

Blast into outer space with this spectacular pull-the-tab rocket craft!

Use the QR code to access the template you need.

WHAT YOU NEED:

- Assorted cardstock/card
- Felt-tip pens or pencils

TOOLS:

- Pair of scissors
- Strong craft glue

1 Print, copy, or trace the shapes from the template onto the specified materials and cut out.

2 Fold the pull strip along the dotted lines indicated on the template and glue down all folds except for the tabs – leave them raised up as shown.

3 Turn the back board so that the back is facing you. Glue the guide to the back board above the slot.

4 Thread the tabs from the pull strip into the slot in the back board.

5 Glue the guide over the pull strip so that it can still move up and down.

6 Glue together the layers of flame and smoke in size order as shown.

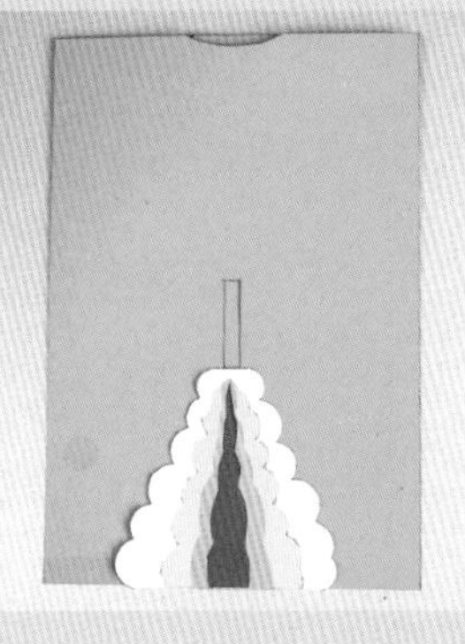

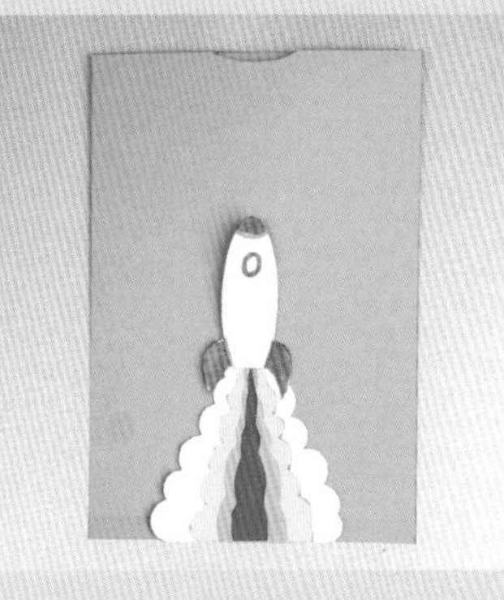

7 Flip the back board over, then place the flames over the middle of the slot. Glue the furthest edges to the back board.

8 Decorate your rocket with felt-tip pens and pencils. Then, glue it to the top of the flames.

9 Cover the lower part of the flames with the grass, gluing it to the back board at each side, where indicated above.

PULL THE TAB TO LAUNCH THE ROCKET!

ROBO-DOG

Robo-dog is the perfect companion for space travel. Would you explore faraway planets and galaxies with this four-legged friend?

WHAT YOU NEED:

- 2 small craft corks
- Aluminum/silver foil
- Plastic cup
- Small metal nut
- Corrugated cardboard
- Jumbo paper clips
- Plastic eyes

TOOLS:

- Ruler
- Needle pliers
- Wire cutters
- Strong craft glue
- Craft drill
- Pencil and eraser
- Sticky tape

1 Take the two corks and cover with aluminum/silver foil. Secure in place with craft glue.

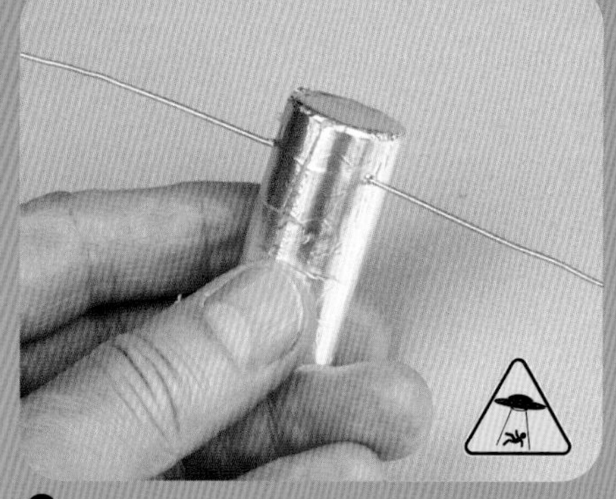

2 Ask an adult to straighten out a jumbo paper clip and push it through the cork about 3 inches (75mm) from one end.

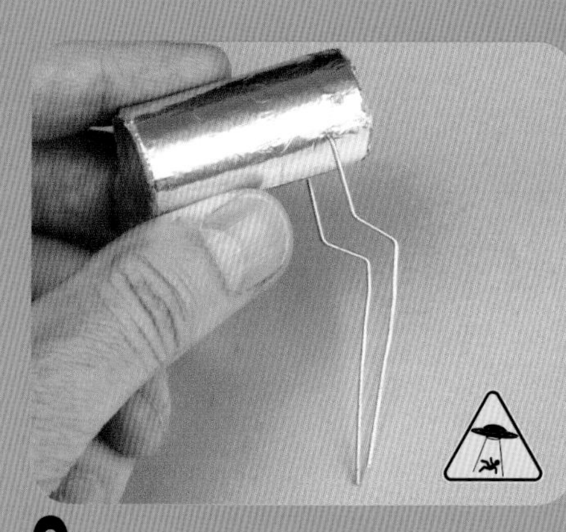

3 Use pliers to shape the wire downward to make rear legs.

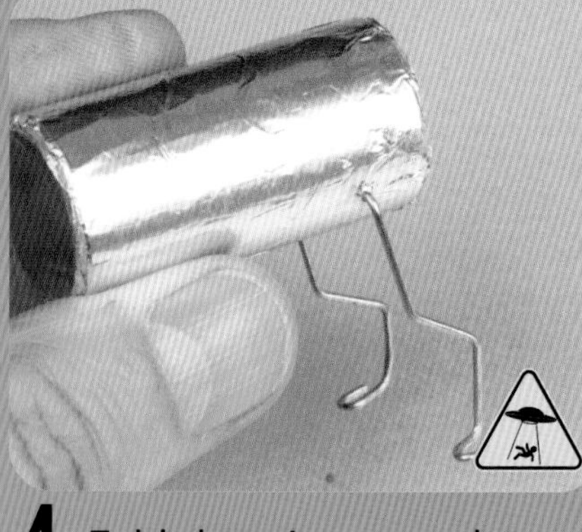

4 Fold the wire around to make knees and paws. Snip off any excess wire.

5 Repeat steps 2-4 at the front of the cork to make front legs.

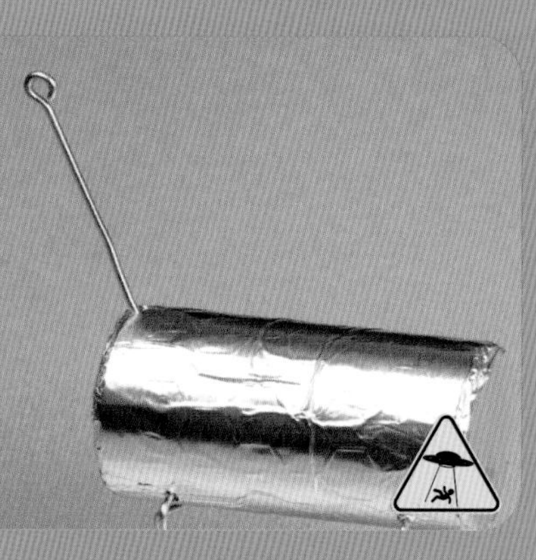

6 Add a small loop to a straightened out paper clip to make a tail. Set aside the body until step 9.

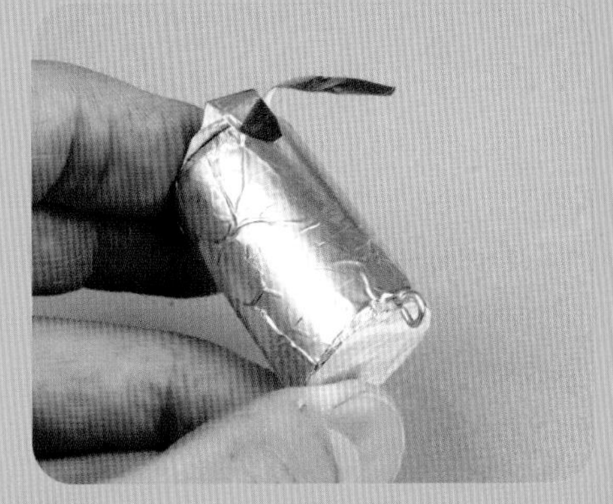

7 Use a double thickness of foil to make the dog ears. Then, glue the ears to the back of the second cork.

8 Turn the cork so that the ears are at the back, then fold them forward a little to make them more realistic.

FOLLOW THESE STEPS TO MAKE IT STAND!

Follow step 9 below if you want to make a mini standing Robo-dog model. Skip straight to step 10 (on page 82) if you want to make it move instead!

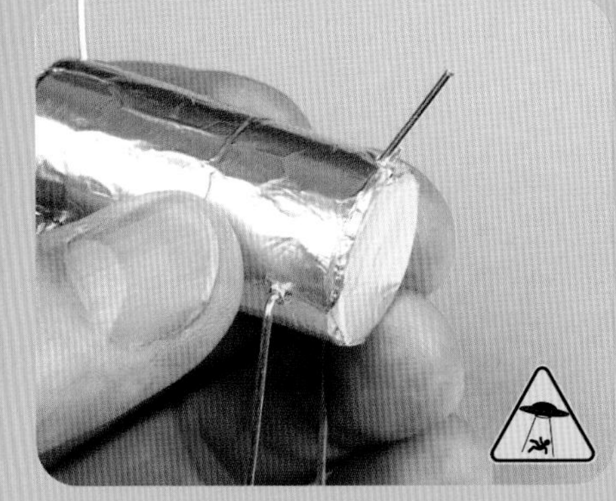

9 Add a short length of wire from a paper clip to the front of the body to make a neck.

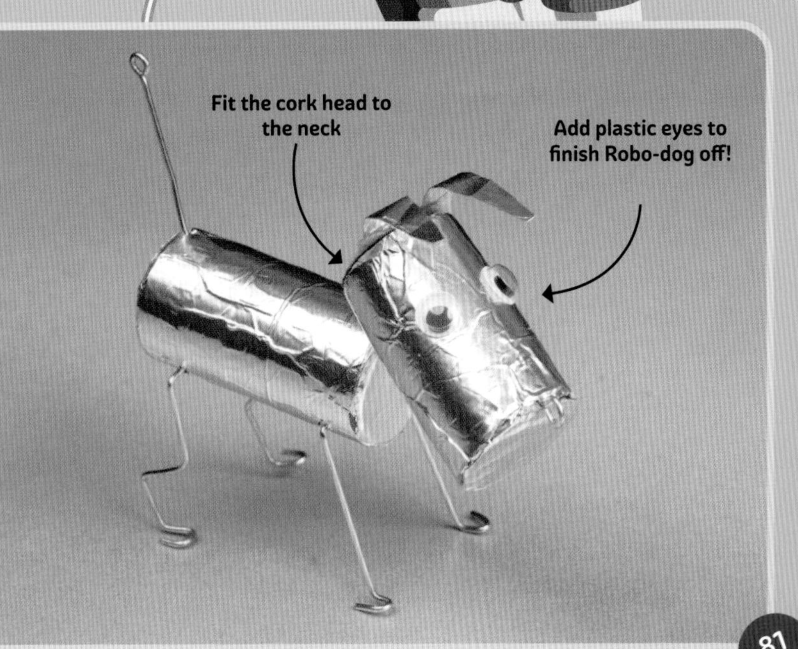

FOLLOW THESE STEPS TO MAKE IT MOVE!

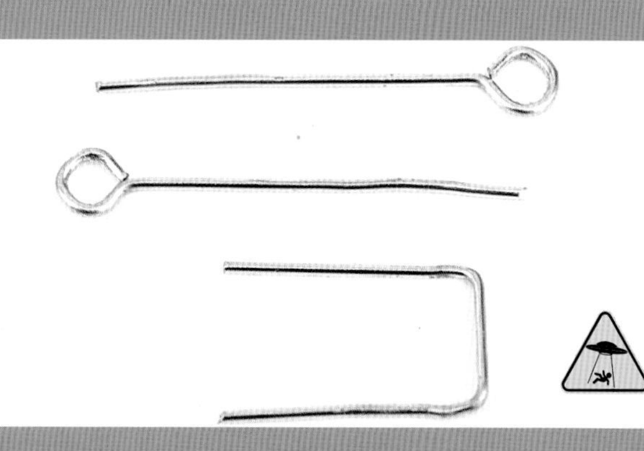

10 Ask an adult to make these wire pieces from an unfolded paper clip using pliers.

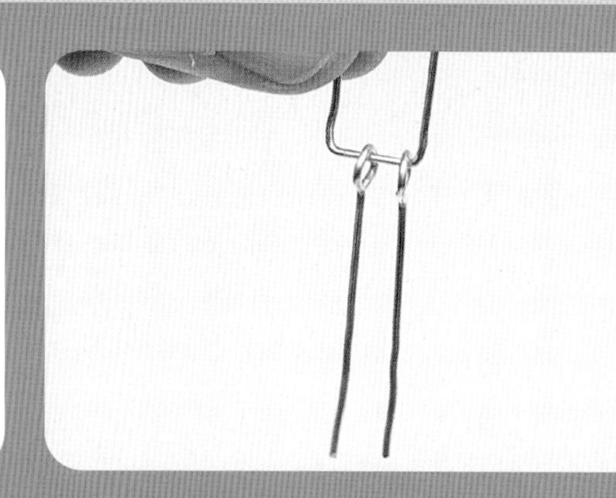

11 Thread the loops into the "U" shape to make into the neck staple.

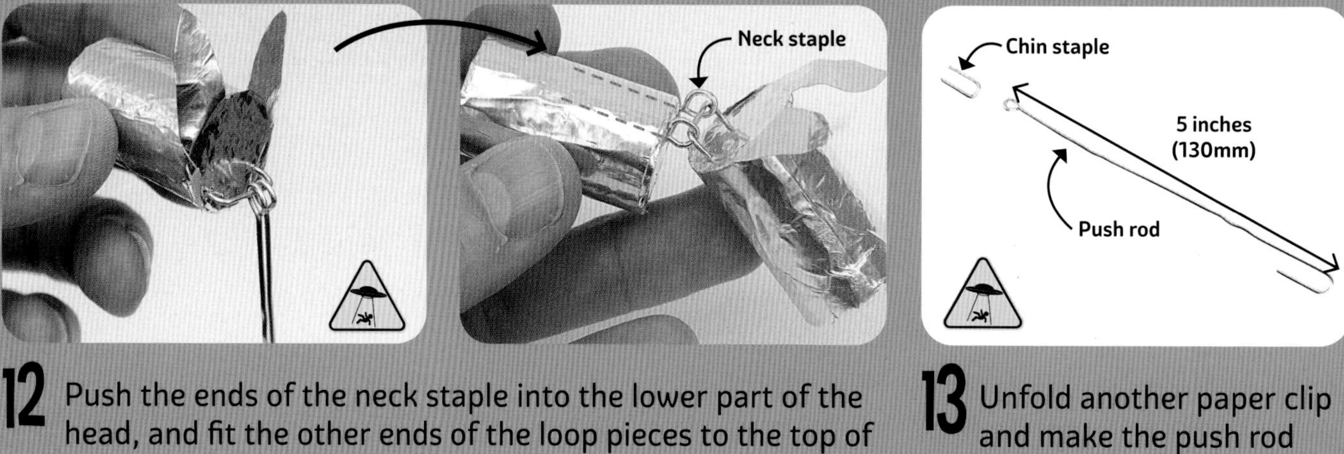

12 Push the ends of the neck staple into the lower part of the head, and fit the other ends of the loop pieces to the top of the body so that the head is free to move up and down.

13 Unfold another paper clip and make the push rod pieces as shown. Cut off a 2 inch (50mm) piece for the chin staple.

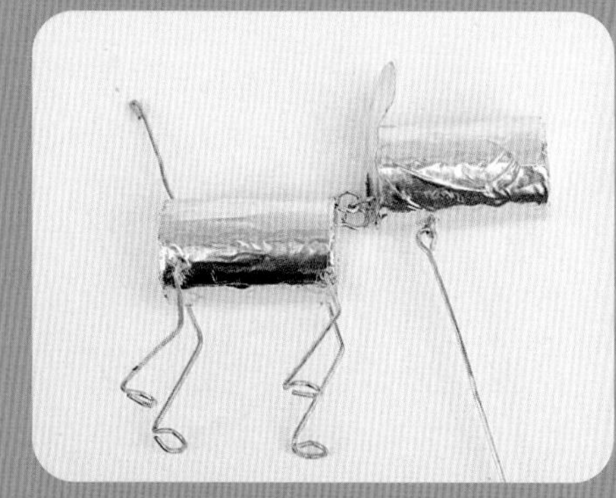

14 Hook the push rod over the chin staple. Push the chin staple into the dog's chin. Set Robo-dog aside until step 18.

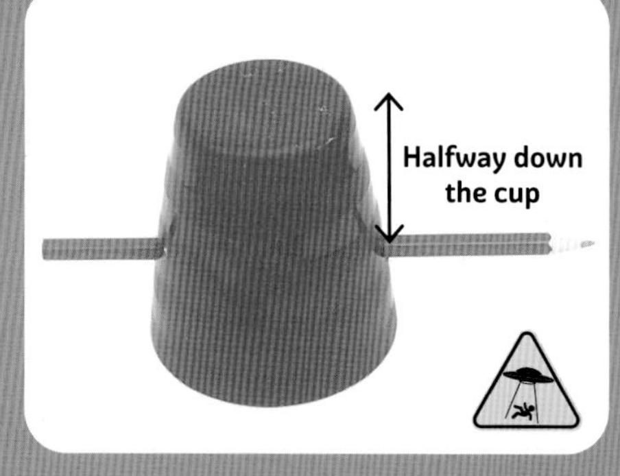

15 Drill holes in opposite sides of the cup, halfway down. Make them big enough for the pencil to fit through.

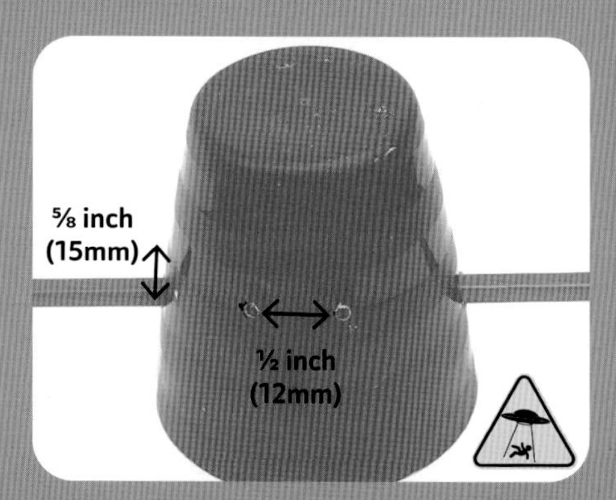

16 Drill two smaller holes in between the pencil holes. They should be ⅝ inch (15mm) above these and ½ inch (12mm) apart.

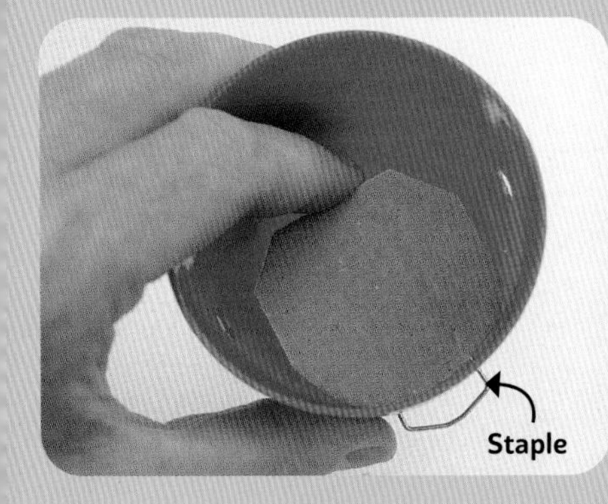

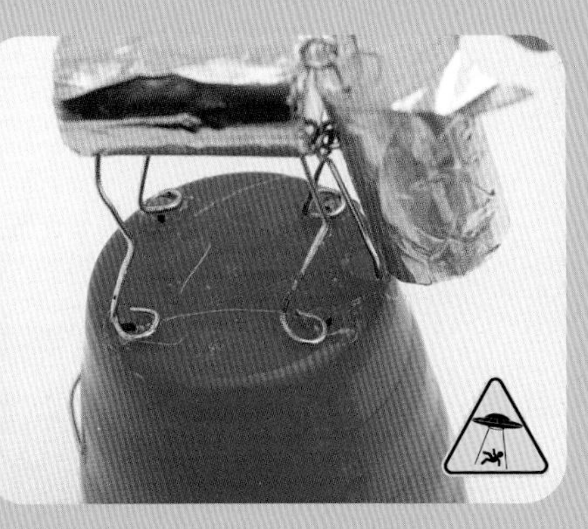

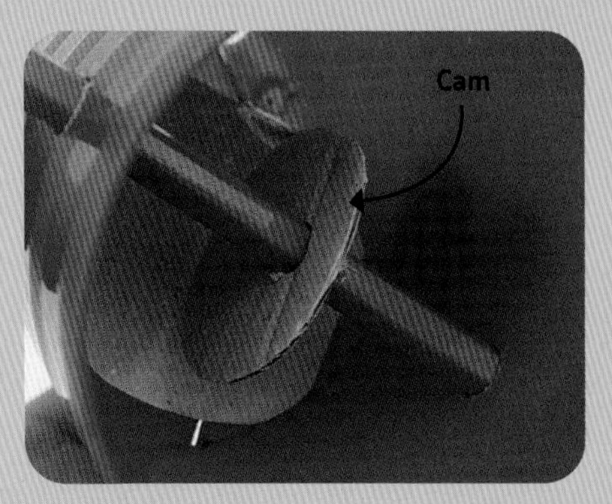

17 Cut out a rough cardboard circle. Use a paper clip to make a staple for the cup. Push it through the small holes in the cup. Then, push it through the cardboard as shown.

18 Place Robo-dog on the upside-down cup, mark where its feet are and drill a hole between the front feet. Thread the push rod through, then glue each foot down in place.

19 Tape the push rod to the cardboard circle. Make a cam from a 1 ¼ inch (30mm) circle of cardboard, with a hole in the middle (see page 11).

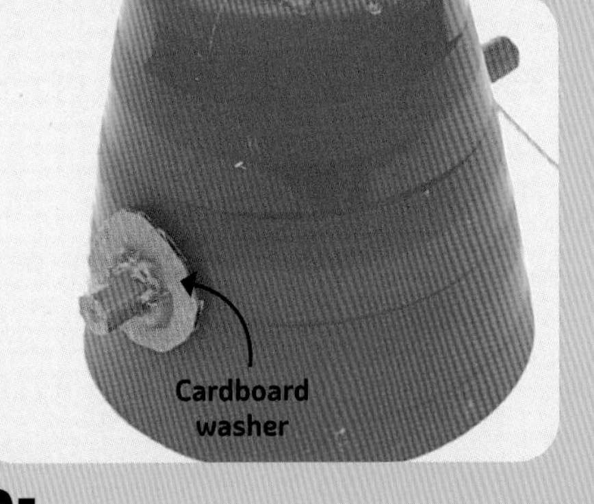

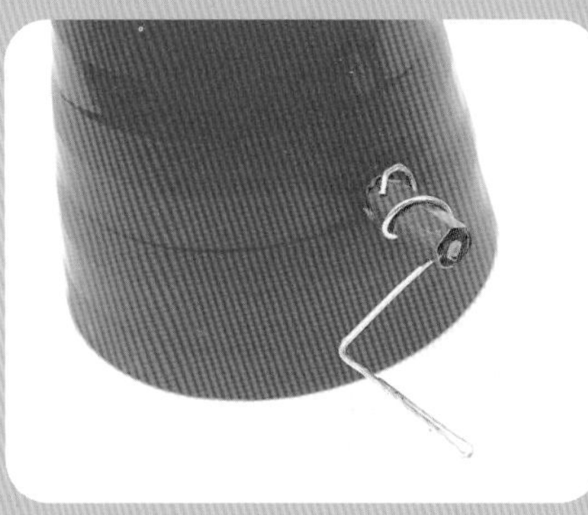

20 Thread the pencil into the cup and cam as shown. Cut the pencil so that ¾ inch (20mm) remains at each side of the cup.

21 Make a 1 inch (25mm) cardboard washer. Add it to the left end of the pencil as Robo-dog faces you.

22 Straighten a paper clip and wrap one end around the right end of the pencil. Shape the rest into a handle.

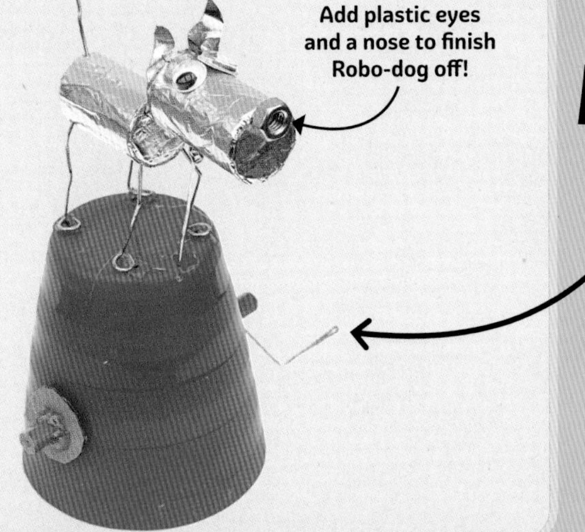

TWIST THE HANDLE TO MAKE ROBO-DOG MOVE!

STARRY NIGHT

TOP TIP

If you don't have a paintbrush, you could use a glue spreader/ spatula, sponges, or even your fingers!

Let's make an impressionist print based loosely on the famous painting 'Starry Night' by Van Gogh. Take a peek at the real deal on page 85 for inspiration before you start!

WHAT YOU NEED:

- Cutting board – larger than your piece of paper
- Assorted plain paper
- Aluminum/ silver foil
- Sticky tape
- Poster paints

TOOLS:

- Pair of scissors
- Wooden stirrers
- Paintbrush

1 Cover one side of the cutting board with aluminum/silver foil. Then, place the paper you want to print onto in the middle of the foil. Stick tape around the edges, but be careful it doesn't touch or hold the paper down. Lift the paper away to reveal a frame for your print area.

2 Scoop out the paints using a wooden stirrer and use the edge of the foil outside the print area as a mixing area.

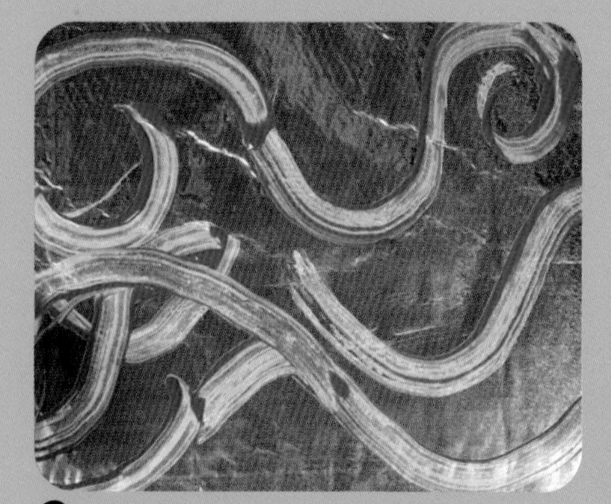

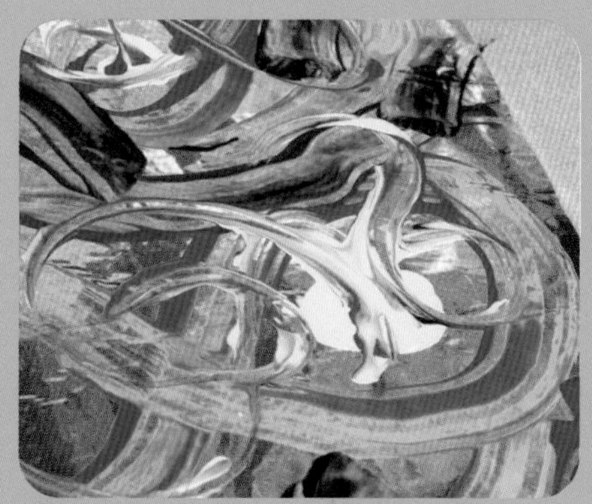

3 Make expressive swirls of paint to fill the foil. Mix blue paint with black or white to change how dark the sky is.

4 Use yellow paint to make stars on the foil. Swirl the paints together to mix them into an explosion of shades and patterns.

5 Once happy with your design, carefully place your paper over the print area. Try not to let it slide side to side as you do so.

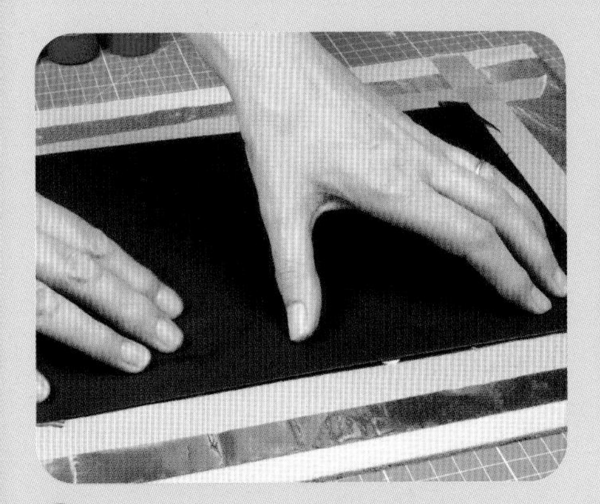

6 Press down over the whole area to transfer the paint to the paper.

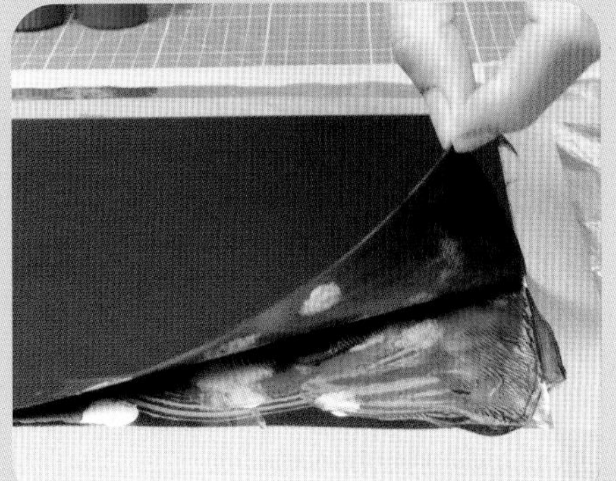

7 Start in one corner and carefully peel the paper off the foil to reveal your masterpiece!

TOP TIP

To clean your paintbrush between using different paints, swish in a paper cup filled with plain water, and dry on a paper towel.

BE CREATIVE! EXPERIMENT WITH DIFFERENT PAPER, TOOLS, AND PAINTS!

'Starry Night' by Van Gogh

ORIGAMI SPACE ROCKET

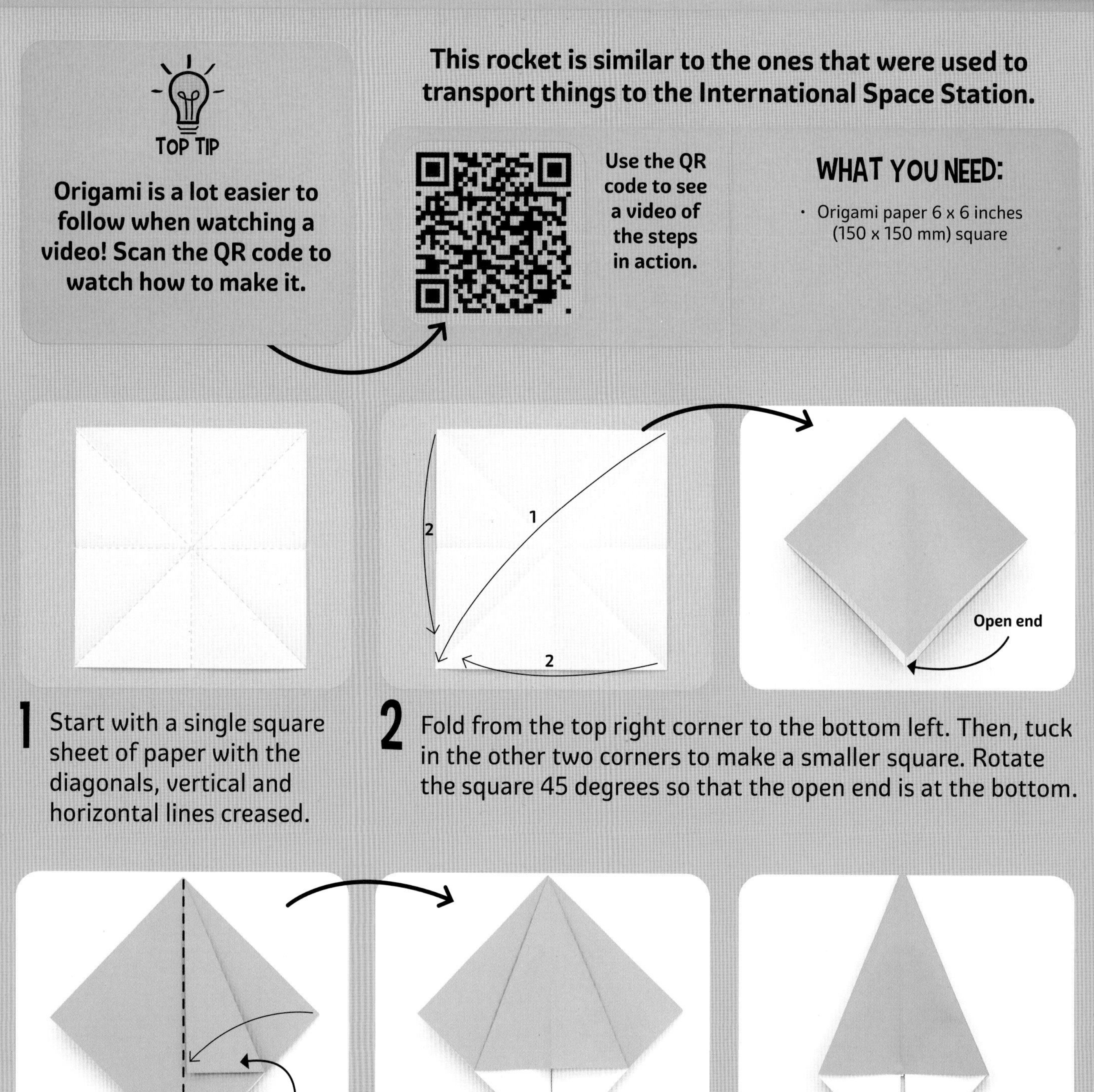

TOP TIP

Origami is a lot easier to follow when watching a video! Scan the QR code to watch how to make it.

This rocket is similar to the ones that were used to transport things to the International Space Station.

Use the QR code to see a video of the steps in action.

WHAT YOU NEED:

- Origami paper 6 x 6 inches (150 x 150 mm) square

1 Start with a single square sheet of paper with the diagonals, vertical and horizontal lines creased.

2 Fold from the top right corner to the bottom left. Then, tuck in the other two corners to make a smaller square. Rotate the square 45 degrees so that the open end is at the bottom.

3 Fold in the right corner to the middle line to create a crease. Pull the lower flap out from underneath (by inserting your fingers under the folded area). Open out and flatten the fold by pulling the flap to the bottom left edge to make an inverted kite shape. Crease the paper in place.

4 Flip the paper over and repeat step 3 three more times with the other flaps, until it looks like the image above.

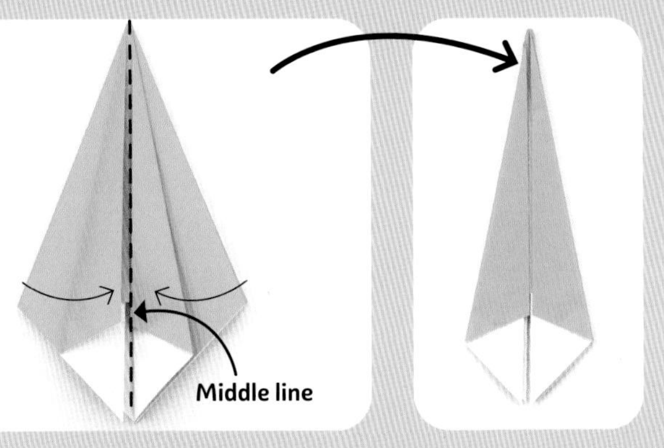

Rocket fin

5 Fold the outer left and right corners to the vertical middle line and crease along the fold. Flip the paper over and repeat three more times with the other flaps.

6 Lift up the bottom flap, fold it in on itself, and pull the foot out to make a rocket fin.

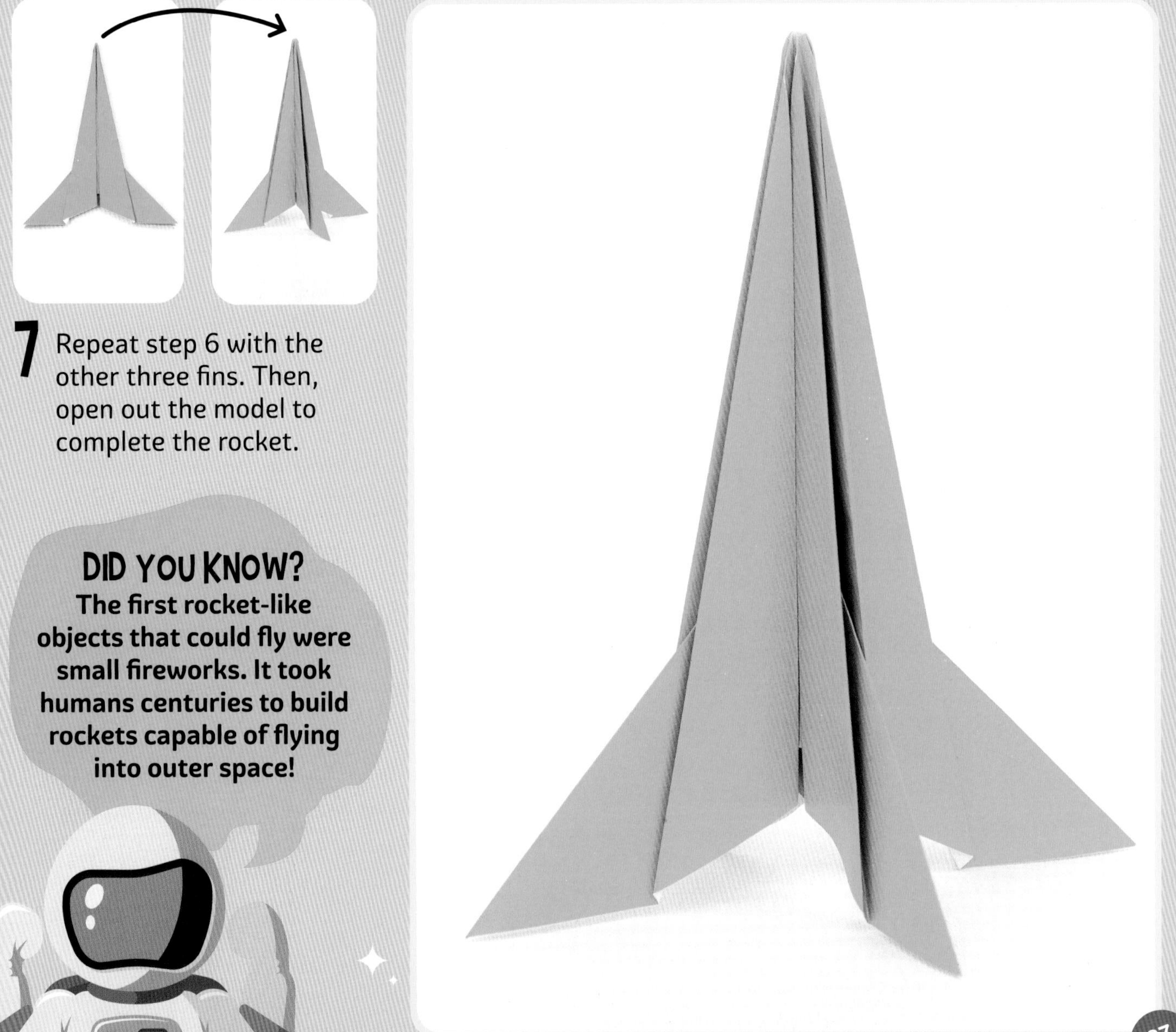

7 Repeat step 6 with the other three fins. Then, open out the model to complete the rocket.

DID YOU KNOW?

The first rocket-like objects that could fly were small fireworks. It took humans centuries to build rockets capable of flying into outer space!

COMET CARD

Impress your friends and family with this amazing moving card. Open and close it to watch the comet soar over the Earth.

Use the QR code to access the template you need.

WHAT YOU NEED:

- Assorted cardstock/card
- 2 pieces of stiff black cardstock/card
- White paint marker pen
- Felt-tip pens or pencils

TOOLS:

- Ruler
- Pair of scissors
- Strong craft glue

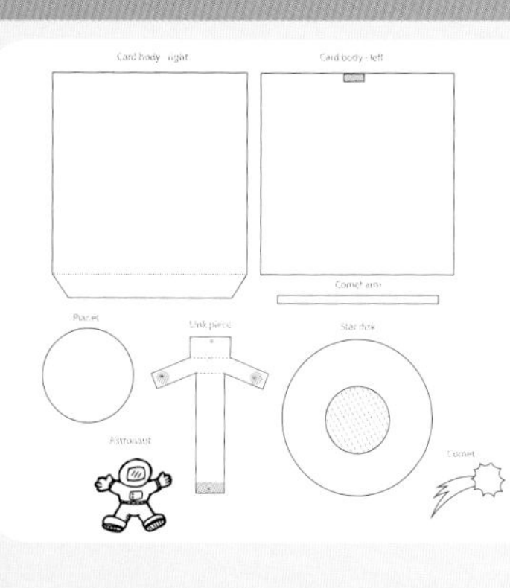

1 Print, copy, or trace the shapes from the templates onto the specified materials and cut out.

2 Decorate the comet and planet with felt-tip pens, pencils, or different bits of cardstock/card.

3 Use a white paint marker pen to add a starry field background to the ring.

4 Glue the two black cardstock/card squares from the template together to make one large card. Fold along the middle crease, then open out again.

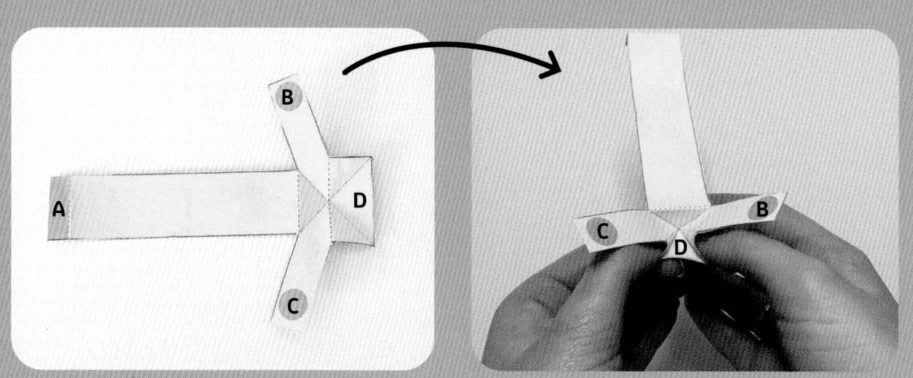

5 Take the link piece and fold along the lines indicated on the template to create creases. Use the images above to see how to fold the link piece correctly. Our link piece is bright to make the steps easier for you to follow, but you should use black cardstock/card for the best effect.

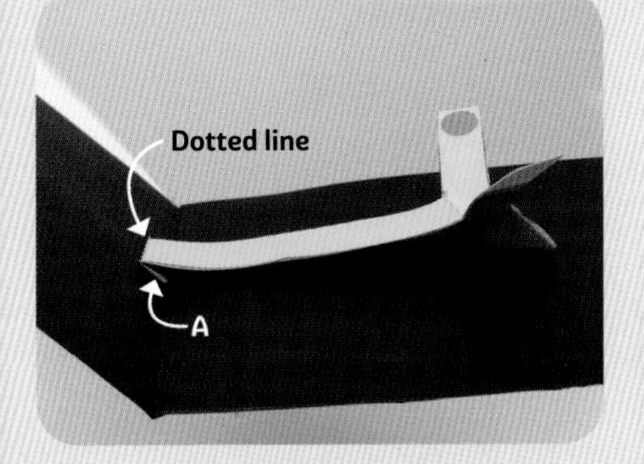

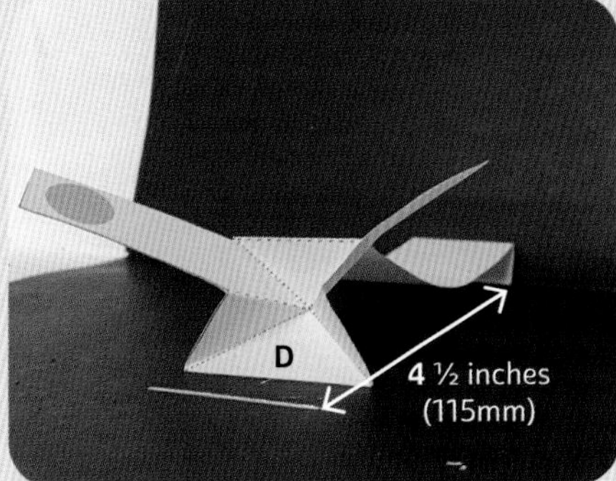

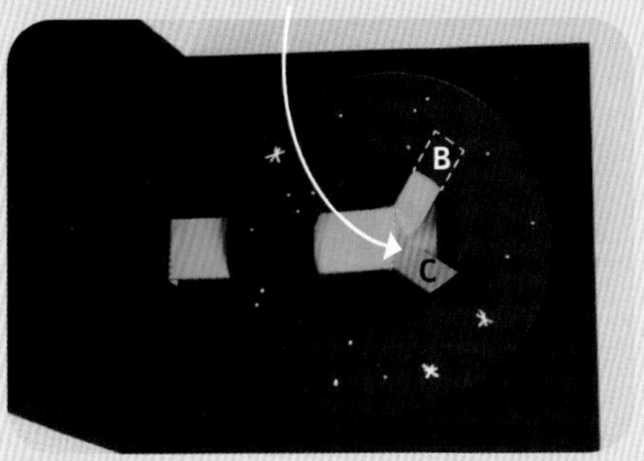

6 Fold section A on the link piece along the dotted line. Add glue to section A, then stick the flap to the inside cover as shown.

7 Mark a line 4 ½ inches (115mm) from the card crease. Add glue to the back of section D, pull it to the line and press down.

8 Add glue to the tip of section B on the link piece. Thread the ring into the position shown to stick the ring to section B.

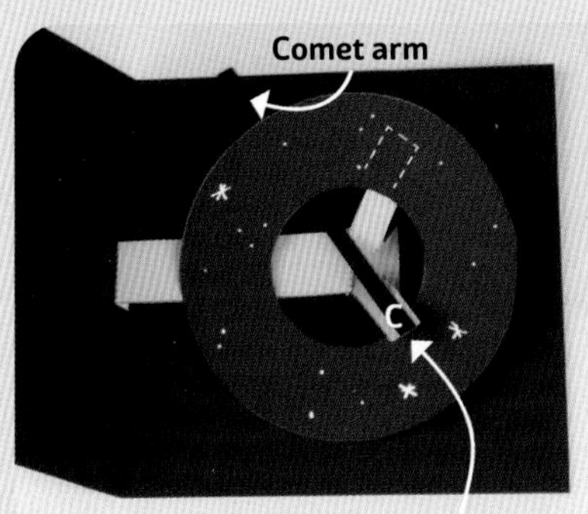

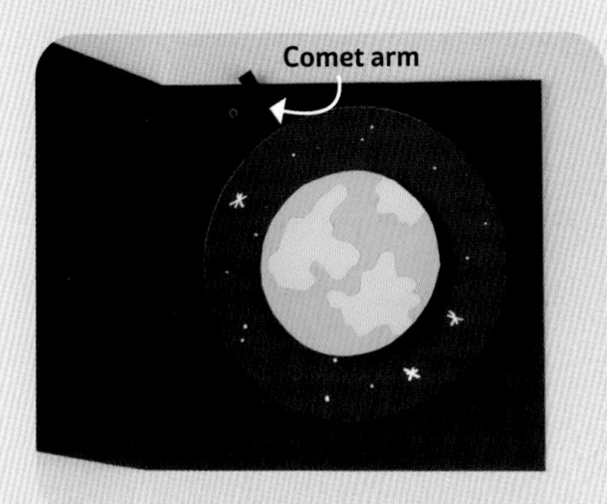

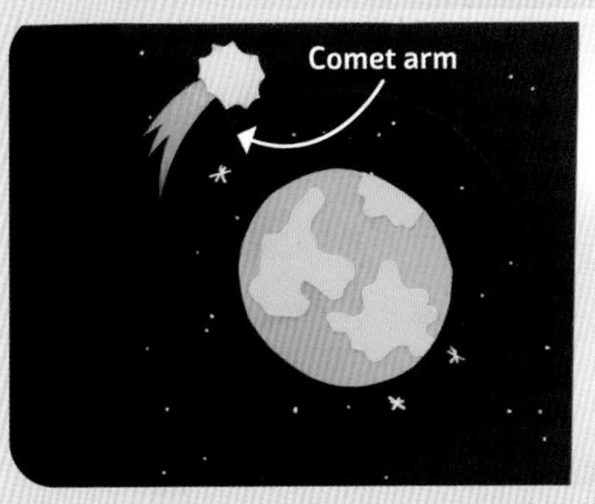

9 Thread the comet arm through the ring hole. Line it up with section C and glue the tips of each together as shown.

10 Place the planet over the ring so that it's directly over the middle of the hole, then glue the back of the planet to section C.

11 Glue your comet to the top of the comet arm. Then, add a few more stars to the background to complete your card.

12 Decorate the front of your card to finish it off! Use the astronaut template or draw your own design.

DID YOU KNOW?

Scientists name comets, usually after the person or spacecraft that discovered them. They've discovered thousands of different comets!

DID YOU KNOW?

Comets are giant snowballs made of frozen gas, rock, and dust. As they get close to the Sun, they heat up. This makes it looks like they're glowing and creates the long tail they're known for.

OPEN AND CLOSE YOUR CARD TO SEE THE COMET FLY OVER EARTH!

GLOSSARY

Aerodynamics – the study of how air moves around a solid object. The more aerodynamic an object is, the better it will fly.

Astronomer – a scientist who studies outer space.

Astronomical - something which is to do with astronomy, the study of all objects outside Earth's atmosphere (see below).

Earth's atmosphere – layers of gases surrounding Earth which are held in place by gravity (see right).

Escape velocity – the constant velocity (speed and direction) needed for an object to escape from a planet's gravitational pull.

Galaxy – a huge collection of gas, dust, and billions of stars and their solar systems, all held together by gravity (see right).

Gravity - a pulling force that works across space. Objects don't have to touch each other for gravity to affect them. For example, the Sun, which is millions of miles away, pulls on Earth and the other planets and objects in the solar system to keep them in orbit.

Intelligent life – living beings that can think, learn, and understand things.

International Space Station (ISS) – a large spacecraft in Earth's orbit which is used as a base for scientific research.

NASA – the National Aeronautics and Space Administration is an agency that deals with space research and exploration. They're based in the USA.

Orbit – the repeated path taken by one object circling around another object in space.

Satellite – any object that orbits a planet. Satellites can be natural, like moons, or artificial (man-made items), like the communications satellites we use to send phone calls and TV signals, and for weather forecasting!

Spacewalk – when an astronaut spends time outside the spacecraft while in outer space. They do this to repair spacecraft and satellites, and carry out scientific experiments.

Star field – a region of the sky containing stars as seen in a telescope or photograph.

Thrust – the force that pushes something in a particular direction. For example, the power of a rocket's engine pushes the spacecraft forward.

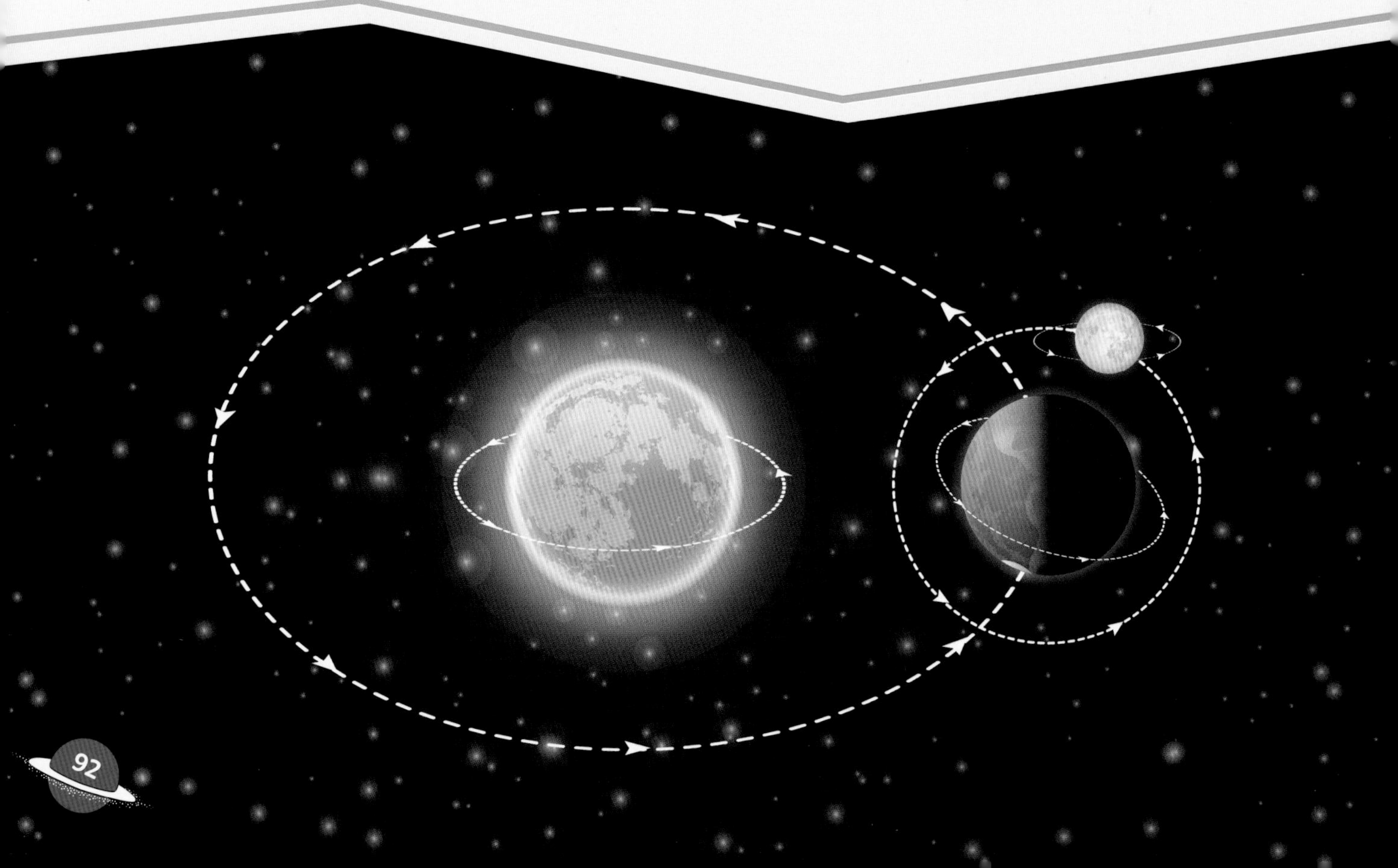

INDEX

PICTURE CREDITS:

(Abbreviations: t=top, b=bottom, m=middle, l=left, r=right, bg=background)

Shutterstock: Digital Images Studio 38-39; Dima Zel 45b; Fast_ Cyclone (illustrated throughout – safety icons); FishCoolish (illustrated throughout – astronaut characters); Franco Tognariuni 23b; Helen Dream 32b; Lukasz Payl Szczepanski 30-31b; M.Aurelius 70b; Marko Aliaksandr 90-91bg; Muratart 59b; NASA images 12b; Paulista 50-51b; Sergey Nivens 4-5bg, 36b; Siberian Art 56b; Spatuletain 85b; Tartila (individual planets) 2-3, 68, 94-95; Triff 27b; Urvana 52b; Vadim Sadovski 69b; Vovan 21mr.

THE AUTHOR

Rob Ives is a UK-based designer and paper engineer. A former teacher, he now works on paper animations and science projects, and often visits schools to talk about design technology and demostrate his models. His published titles include *Paper Models That Rock!*, *Paper Automata*, and the *Build it! Make it!* series (below).

CHECK OUT OTHER BOOKS IN THE SERIES: